Time Out for Happiness

Time Out for Happiness

Frank B. Gilbreth, Jr.

THOMAS Y. CROWELL COMPANY   NEW YORK
Established 1834

DESIGNED BY VIRGINIA SMITH

Manufactured in the United States of America

L. C. Card 73-142192
ISBN 0-690-82517-X

2 3 4 5 6 7 8 9 10

Contents

Acknowledgments

Aside from my own recollections, the two main sources of material for this book were my mother's privately printed booklet, *The Quest of the One Best Way,* and Edna Yost's splendid biography of my parents, *Frank and Lillian Gilbreth, Partners for Life,* originally published in 1949 by the Rutgers University Press, New Brunswick, New Jersey.

I also relied on various scientific books by my parents; on *The Writings of the Gilbreths,* edited by William R. Spriegel and Clark E. Myers, published in 1953 by Richard D. Irwin, Inc., of Homewood, Illinois; on a diary which my mother kept while teaching in the Philippines and subsequently sent to me; and on letters from her to me dating back to my college days.

Most of the data on the confrontation between the Taylor and Gilbreth systems came from the Yost book and from a paper by Milton J. Nadworny entitled *Frederick Taylor and Frank Gilbreth: Competition in Scientific Management.*

Reminiscences by friends of my father, published in 1968 by the American Society of Mechanical Engineers at a centennial anniversary of his birth, were valuable source material.

My cousin, Caroline C. Hasty, furnished much of the material on my father's family background. She also made available to me a handwritten booklet of reminiscences by our mutual grandmother, Martha Bunker Gilbreth, and scrapbooks kept by her.

My brothers and sisters read the manuscript and were helpful. My mother herself read the first third of the book, covering her girlhood and courtship. Her health failed before I completed the final two-thirds.

Time Out for Happiness

CHAPTER 1

The Shy Redhead and Mister Man

You could hardly have found a more unlikely candidate for the job Lillie Gilbreth inherited: raising a big brood of children on a shoestring and becoming a "female engineer."

As a young woman, she had thought she'd always be a spinster. And since her family was wealthy and she was sheltered, it certainly never occurred to her that the time would come when she'd be scratching for a living in a man's world —with a dozen mouths to feed.

Even when I first remember her—shortly before World War I when I was four or five years old and she was in her late thirties—she was utterly unprepared for the task she later fell heir to.

She couldn't cook, never had done any laundry, didn't know much about sewing or knitting, and never had run a house of her own, since that last function was performed by a blunt, if well-meaning, mother-in-law. Yet every washing machine, kitchen stove, and refrigerator that rolls off the assembly lines today bears the imprint of her research.

She couldn't drive an automobile, didn't know a Stillson from a monkey wrench, and was baffled by such things as slide rules and simple quadratic equations. My father used to allege that she once threatened to call the S.P.C.A. when she heard a carpenter say he'd file a keyhole with a rat-tail. Yet she became an outstanding engineer in a pioneering field.

She was so shy that she wasn't at all keen about appearing in public. She dreaded making speeches, even though she *had* made the Commencement Day talk for her graduating class at the University of California. She was terribly nervous in automobiles, and became sick almost as soon as she walked up the gangplank of a boat. Not being able to swim, she was nervous in boats. Yet she became an accomplished speaker who traveled a hundred thousand miles and more a year, meeting lecture engagements around the world.

Back in those days, she was happiest in the warm, if sometimes riotously noisy, bosom of her family, where her mother-in-law and a half-dozen servants took care of the mundane affairs. Sometimes my plump and boisterous father would reach over and squeeze her hand, and even that much attention in the presence of us children would make her blush and smile self-consciously.

At that time, Lillie and Frank were blessed—if that's the verb I want—with only six or seven of us. Often we'd insist that she play the piano for us, but although she had studied music in college she was never too keen to comply. I suppose the reason was that my father's sister, Aunt Anne, was a professional, and Lillie felt her efforts would sound amateurish to my father and his mother.

She sounded first-rate to us, though, especially when she'd sing to her own accompaniment.

" 'Backward, turn backward, oh time in thy flight,' " she'd intone sadly in her none-too-confident soprano—and I'd have to wink back tears of pity, because anyone past thirty seemed so hopelessly old. " 'Make me a chi-eld again, just for tonight.' "

"Do you think we ought to keep *that* one—the one with all those freckles and the bleary eyes?" my father asked her on one occasion, as he pointed to me when she had finished.

"I should *so say,*" she assured me warmly, since she didn't believe in teasing children.

"You're sure?" he persisted. "Shouldn't we turn him in for a new model? Do you *really* want to keep him?"

"You shouldn't talk like that," Lillie reprimanded him, and it was one of the few times I ever heard her do so. "Look at him. He thinks you mean it."

"Your trouble, Boss," he told her—and although he often called her that, he didn't fool anybody, because really it was the other way around—"is that you don't have a sense of humor."

Although that certainly wasn't true, Lillie didn't bother to argue it. "Maybe not, dear," she conceded, without a trace of irritation or martyrdom, and without indulging in the luxury of what was known in those days as a snappy comeback —perhaps to the effect that in order to live with him a woman would *have* to possess a sense of humor.

Although she seemed old to me in those days when she was asking time to turn backward and make her a chi-eld, she also seemed beautiful. But by her own appraisal, confided to a diary, she was pathetically plain. When I look back at photographs and try to view them impartially, I still think the appraisal is nearer my extreme than hers.

She had straight, red-brown hair that she wore up, but could hang to her waist when she let it. Her eyes were blue-green and extraordinarily bright. Her mouth, if not exactly generous, would still in all fairness have to be called unselfish.

Lillie disliked her nose, which was sharp and thin—but still entirely acceptable and somewhat aristocratic looking. Years later, when her nose was crushed in an auto accident, she had it set duller and wider—and was childishly pleased with it.

She was agile and slim (except, of course, when she was expecting a baby), a little taller than average, and she stood straight with her head up and shoulders back. Just the same, there was a slight air of apology about her bearing. It was more unaggressiveness, I suppose, than any feeling of inferiority. Whatever the reason, we bullied her more than we should have. I know I felt I could wrap her around my finger, and get anything I wanted. But, remember, I'm still talking about those early days. Later, her air of apology disappeared altogether, and so did her toleration of bullies.

She was gentle, and never so much as raised her voice at children, let alone shook, pinched, or spanked them. And this was all the more remarkable in view of the fact that each of us was thoroughly competent to try a saint. Acting in concert, I'm sure we had all the necessary attributes to try a whole cloudful of them.

Certainly our neighbors found us trying. For instance, there was an occasion when two of our neighbors were talking, and one of them noticed smoke coming from a window of our house.

"Good God, the Gilbreths' house is on fire!" he exclaimed. "I'd better call the fire department."

The other neighbor looked at him incredulously. "Call

the fire department and have them put it *out?*" he asked, shaking his head. "Are you crazy?"

The fire turned out to be a false alarm, anyway. The smoke was from some flashlight powder my father was using to take still-pictures of the family. No one ever lived who had the courage to use more flashlight powder per exposure than he, and the shattering explosions had been known to break windows and remove huge chunks of plaster from the ceilings. When he so much as took a lens cap off a camera, the family dogs and cats would take cover, the young children would start bellowing, and the older children would instinctively put their hands over their heads for protection against flying debris.

On another occasion, which didn't have anything to do with flash guns, a next-door neighbor at Nantucket, Massachusetts, where we spent the summers, told my father point-blank that while he liked all of us and wanted to remain friends, he simply couldn't stand the noise, and intended to move.

"He'll never do it," Dad told us. "He's too fond of that old house of his. But he's really awfully nice, and we're going to have to be more quiet for him."

The neighbor wasn't bluffing, though. The next day a construction crew came out, jacked up the house, and moved it all the way down to the tip of Brant Point, a distance of close to a mile, where it still stands.

"I've heard that Arabs do it all the time," my father used to mutter enviously as he observed the empty homesite next door. "Sometimes when you kids are howling I wish I could fold *my* tent and silently . . ."

Instead of trying to boss her children, Mother always treated us as equals. And, all her life, she was a *listener.* Even if an exceptionally dull adult or a three-year-old child were speaking to her, she'd give him the courtesy of her un-divided attention.

For his part, Dad believed in laying down the law unilat-erally, and in loud and no uncertain terms. And although he was a pretty fair listener himself, and believed in submitting some problems to a Family Council, he also thought it was a grave mistake to spare the rod—or at any rate the switch.

"Speak loudly and carry a small stick," he once advised Mother.

Needless to say, she could manage us much better than he could. And although we *could* bully her into giving us what we wanted, we wouldn't have dreamed of defying her or hurting her in any way.

Sometimes the pressures of a big family, a loving but tem-peramental husband, and an almost equally loving but blunt mother-in-law became too much for Lillie. Then her shoul-ders would start to shake, and she'd hold a handkerchief to her face as she tried to slip unnoticed to her bedroom. She'd close the door, but we could still hear the quiet sobs she couldn't quite restrain.

Frank would look bewildered as he hurried to comfort her, and the rest of us would ask each other belligerently who had been guilty of breaking our poor old mother's heart.

Later, when she had control of herself again, she'd emerge red-eyed, and apologize to us.

"I don't really mind noise," she'd tell us. "You can make all the noise you want, and it doesn't bother me. But it has to be happy noise. It can't be fighting noise. I just can't stand fighting. I'm sorry. It's the only thing I can't stand."

That wasn't quite the whole truth, either, because another thing she couldn't stand, back in those days, was lightning. Since she was in the process of getting her Ph.D. in psychology, she knew it would be a bad example to let us know of her fear. But on more than one occasion, as claps of thunder rumbled, we caught her in a dark closet holding her ears.

Frank, in many ways, was her exact opposite. Where she had been reared in luxury, his mother had run a boarding-house. Where she was slim and shy, he was plump and gregarious. Far from being afraid of lightning, he enjoyed walking in the rain and trying to pick up the flashes through binoculars. I only heard him cry once in my life, and that was a single, almost inaudible whimper as he emerged from a room where his mother had just died.

Lillie and Frank met for the first time in Boston in 1903. Lillian Evelyn Moller was en route from her home in California to Europe, for the Grand Tour. She was accompanied by three other young ladies from the West Coast and a schoolteacher chaperone. She was twenty-five years old, wore a Phi Beta Kappa key under her prim lace collar, possessed a master's degree in English literature, was convinced she was a Plain Jane, had filled more than twenty notebooks with sonnets and several diaries with observations, and had never been on an unescorted date with a man in her life.

Frank Bunker Gilbreth, born in Maine and reared in Boston by his widowed mother, was ten years older. He had started work as a bricklayer's apprentice at the age of seventeen, had risen to the top of his company, had gone into business for himself at twenty-six, and had quickly become one of the best-known building contractors in the world.

He was a sandy-haired, outgoing, incredibly energetic bachelor, who had just barely escaped being led to the altar four different times. He was also a fashionable dresser, had branch offices in New York and London, and bought every new-model bicycle and horseless carriage that hit the market.

One reason for his success was that he recognized the country's preoccupation with speed as it entered the twentieth century. Also, he had discovered the value of advertising, and had a knack for keeping his name before the public.

For example, he made headlines by setting speed records in constructing dams, factories, and skyscrapers. Taking some outrageous chances, he'd start moving steel, cement, and bricks toward a construction job even before he had been awarded the contract. Then, once the contract *was* signed, he'd amaze the populace and the newspapers by beginning work that very afternoon. And instead of fighting the unions, he held a union card himself and worked with them.

Sometimes he'd synchronize operations of various work crews by standing on a giant scaffold above the project and issuing orders through a megaphone, for all the world like a college cheerleader.

These maneuvers caught the public fancy. Just a year before he met Lillie, he even made the front pages by building the Lowell Electrical Laboratory at the Massachusetts Institute of Technology in eleven weeks!

Lillie's schoolteacher chaperone, who was showing the four ladies the sights of Boston before they sailed for Europe, happened to be Frank's first cousin. So it was she, Minnie Bunker, who introduced Lillie to Frank. But that wasn't the way he used to tell it to us.

"Did I ever tell you how I first happened to meet your mother?" he'd ask us loudly for her benefit.

Of course he'd told us a hundred times, but we liked to see Mother blush when he teased her, so we'd always reply that it was news to us.

"Well, I was driving along the streets of Boston in my new buzz-wagon, a Winton Six, when I saw this red-haired . . ."

"Blonde," Mother interposed.

". . . this strawberry blonde baby-doll standing on a cor-ner and looking kind of lonesome. I don't know what was the matter with that Winton, but whenever it approached a cunning baby-doll it used to swerve to the curb and stop."

We told him that we'd bet *he* was the one who made the car swerve and stop, and that he couldn't josh us.

"I'm not joshing," he continued. "Now if I do say so my-self, I was a pretty handsome fellow in those days. I was thin as a rail—not covered with muscle as I am today."

"Oh, yes indeedy," Mother nodded. "Hmmm!"

"Anyway, after the buzz-wagon stopped, this baby-doll stepped up to the runningboard, flashed me a come-hither smile, and cooed, 'Hello, there, Mister Man. Say, that's a mighty nifty automobile. What about a little ride, Dearie?' "

"And what did you say, Daddy?"

"Well, naturally, my mother had taught me not to talk to strange women, and *especially* never to get in an automobile with one. So I politely suggested to the redhead that she skiddoo. But she winked at me, and . . ."

And so it went. We had long since pumped Cousin Min-nie dry about the *real* circumstances of that first meeting. But it was fun to hear Dad tell it.

"The only part of your story I *really* object to, dear," Mother once told Dad, "is the part about my calling you 'Mister Man.' What a horrible, simpering, coyly coquettish expression! The rest of your story is so outrageous that I'm sure the children don't believe it. Maybe my hair *was* a little on the red side, and maybe I *did* go for a ride in that Winton—although, as I remember, Minnie was along too. But for the record, children, I never called anyone 'Mister Man' in my life, and your father knows it."

"I don't know anything of the kind," Dad snorted. "It cer-tainly wasn't 'Tootsie-Wootsie,' was it?"

"That's even worse!"

"Or 'Sweetie Pie' or 'Precious Lamb'?"

"Ye gads!" said Mother, blushing anyway.

"So you see," he concluded triumphantly, "that leaves 'Mister Man'!"

CHAPTER 2

Frozen Strawberries for Firefly

Lillie was born in Oakland, California, May 24, 1878.
Rutherford B. Hayes was the President of the United States,
and the West was still Wild. Custer had made his last stand
only two years before—the same year that Wild Bill Hickok
was killed by a shot in the back at Deadwood, South Dakota.
But Oakland itself was a thriving, law-abiding city. And Lillie's maternal grandfather, who couldn't, or at any rate
wouldn't, speak a word of English, was the richest man in
town.

Her ancestry was entirely German. All four of her grandparents had emigrated to this country in the early 1840's, to
escape hard times in the old country, and had settled originally in New York.

Her maternal grandfather was named Frederick Delger.
He was born in Colditz, Saxony, and learned the trade of

bootmaker before he came to this country as a young man. In New York he met Ernestine Blecher, a twenty-year-old native of Darmstadt, and they were married in 1850. Two years later, Frederick and Ernestine sailed around Cape Horn with their infant daughter, Matilda. When they walked down the gangplank of the square-rigger at San Francisco, Frederick had exactly a dollar in his pocket.

Those were the gold rush days, and if there was anything the California miners needed it was boots. Frederick started to produce them in what, for those days, was almost an assembly-line operation. He also ordered ready-mades from back East. Within a couple of years, he had two shoe stores in San Francisco and one in Sacramento.

Meanwhile, he was investing his profits in real estate, including a few acres which were to become the heart of downtown Oakland.

Eight years after his arrival in California, he was able to sell his shoe stores and retire in Oakland. By that time, besides young Matilda, there were three other children— Annie, who was my mother's mother, Edward, and Lillian.

The most interesting of these was Lillian, for whom my mother was named. She shocked Oakland society by divorcing her husband when she was middle-aged, entering the medical school at Palo Alto, and becoming a doctor. Then she studied with Freud and became a pioneer psychiatrist.

Aunt Lillian got married again—this time happily, to Dr. Sweasy Powers. We used to visit their house in White Plains, New York, where they kept room after room of rare and exotic squirrels, some as big as rabbits. Many of them were confined in ceiling-to-floor cages with large treadmills, but others were privileged to roam the premises.

I'm not sure whether the animals merely served as pets or whether they were connected with psychiatry experiments.

But Aunt Lillian was so crazy about squirrels that she seldom went anywhere without one. When she and Uncle Doctor, as we called Sweasy, drove over to our house in Montclair, New Jersey, for Sunday dinner, she'd always bring a favorite with her, and we'd see its alert little head peeking from her webbed handbag, known as a reticule. The poor creature had become so dependent on human company that it would get terribly nervous if left alone, so one of us would be designated as a squirrel-sitter, while Aunt Lillian and Uncle Doctor ate dinner.

Despite her peculiarities, Aunt Lillian had a keen mind and an adventurous spirit. She was tremendously admired by my mother, who nonetheless admitted that it was nerve-racking, when you went to call on her, to have to shoo squirrels off the chandelier and out of the davenport before you could sit down peacefully for a cup of tea.

Rich old Frederick Delger never got over his homesickness for Germany. So as methods of transportation improved, he'd take his family back to the Old Country every year or so, and ship to Oakland trees and shrubbery he remembered from his youth. He planted these in the yard of his estate, which contained a hothouse, conservatories, a man-sized birdhouse, fish ponds, and grottoes, not to mention the residence itself, which sported two elevators.

He insisted that his wife and children speak their "native tongue," as he called German, and because of his influence, most of his grandchildren, including my mother, were brought up to speak the language fluently, and even to write the flowing script.

He turned down two drafts by a citizens' committee to run for mayor of Oakland, and when he finally died in 1898, his obituary in an Oakland newspaper estimated his estate at "three and a half million dollars, likely to be more rather than less." And that didn't include the house with grottoes, either.

As for his wife, Ernestine, she lived until 1908, and remained a hearty, enthusiastic, uninhibited woman, who gestured sweepingly when she talked. She didn't object to her family's speaking English, and in fact did so herself, but with a heavy and comical accent of the Katzenjammer genre. She liked good food, good wine, and a hearty laugh at a funny joke. All of her grandchildren, including Lillie, were fond of her—and a little scared of her, too.

My mother's paternal grandparents were John Moller, who was born in Rader in 1815, and Adelaide Kuhlman, who was born in Aachen in 1819. They had four sons and four daughters, but three of the boys died in infancy, so my mother's father, William, became an only son. The girls were named Margaret, Elizabeth, Matilda, and Johanna.

Like the Delgers, the Mollers were homesick for Germany after they came to this country. John Moller was a sugar importer, and lived in a brownstone house a few doors away from Tiffany's, in New York. He had offices in Wall Street, and enjoyed riding horseback with his children in Central Park.

On one of the trips back to the Vaterland, the Delgers met the Mollers. Later, Mother's parents-to-be—Annie Delger, seventeen, and William Moller, twenty-six—were married in Hamburg.

William was slim, blue-eyed, courtly, and handsome. It was from him that my mother inherited the thin nose she deplored. Although the only surviving boy in a large family, he was anything but spoiled, and always deferred to his womenfolk—first to his mother and sisters, and later to his wife and daughters.

Annie Delger was petite, with dark hair and eyes. Although she was extraordinarily kind and gentle, she also was a genius at getting her own way. Without raising her voice or pouting or being disagreeable, she managed to be waited on, hand and foot, by her husband for as long as *he* lived, and by her children for as long as *she* lived. Her children practically stood in line to see that her wishes were carried out instantly, and there was considerable rivalry among them as to who would be favored to do her chores.

In many ways, Annie was a remarkable woman. My mother's uncanny ability to control and direct children, without so much as a raised finger or a frown, must have been either learned or inherited from Annie.

When Annie's children were especially well behaved, she'd reward them by allowing them to do special favors for *her*.

"Lillie," she told my mother, "from now on, dear, if you like, you can get up early in the morning and pick a nice little bouquet for my breakfast tray."

"Mother taught me what to pick and what not to pick; how I could help the plants stay beautiful," Lillie once wrote. "I was allowed to pick and arrange the flowers for her breakfast tray. It was my job, my privilege. The garden was so beautiful at sunrise. My father's job was watering the garden in the cool of the evening. I loved to help him . . . ."

Yes, Annie Delger must have been a natural-born psychologist. Perhaps she, like her sister who subsequently kept squirrels, should also have studied with Freud.

We children called Annie "Grosie," which was short for the German *grosmutter,* meaning grandmother. Grosie couldn't enter a room without one of my uncles helping her into a chair, another uncle closing a window behind her, an aunt departing with deliberate speed to fetch a shawl, and my mother leaping forward with an assortment of pillows and a lap-rug.

Grosie had a round, merry face, and her eyes would light up with pleasure at all this attention. You could tell she was proud of the manners and thoughtfulness of her offspring, who were then all adults.

As for my brothers and sisters and me, we too found ourselves lowering our voices and minding our manners in her presence, and after a few hours we'd be picking flowers for her and rushing forward with pillows and scarfs, too.

Like my mother, Grosie seldom felt the need of issuing a sharp reprimand. But when she *did* issue one, its very infrequency made it all the more effective.

Lillie used to say that after she was married she was taken to task only once by Grosie—and that it taught her a "needed lesson." But of course no lesson that Grosie taught could be other than needed—in the eyes of Lillie and the other Mollers.

The lesson came on a visit which Lillie made to Oakland in 1917. Grosie gave her a list of six old friends who lived nearby, and suggested that Lillie call on them.

Even a mild suggestion from Grosie was the equivalent to an edict from anybody else. So Lillie dutifully—and despite the fact that she was, as usual, expecting another baby soon —hastened into her best clothes, summoned the chauffeur on the double, and departed under forced draft in one of the Mollers' three Packards.

She returned shortly before supper, and informed Grosie she had managed to polish off all six calls in one afternoon.

"Do you mean, Lillie-dear, that you spent only twenty

minutes or so at each house?" Grosie asked her daughter.

"Yes, Mama-dear. Don't you think I was efficient?"

Efficiency, by then, had become a byword in the Gilbreth household. I suppose it was the most overworked single word in our vocabularies. Grosie apparently had taken due notice of this, and was not altogether pleased. For once there wasn't that merry gleam in her eyes.

"Perhaps, Lillie-dear," she said slowly, "you were a *little* . . . *too* . . . efficient."

And if the reprimand seems mild, at least it was sufficient to straighten out Lillie, who was so crushed she never forgot it.

The record indicates that Grosie lost the initial argument to her husband, in their long and happy marriage—but won every time after that.

The initial argument had to do with where they'd live. Grosie wanted "John's Billy," as her bridegroom was called to distinguish him from various cousins named Billy, to move to Oakland. He wanted to stay in New York, where he was doing well in his father's sugar business down on Wall Street.

So John's Billy won that argument, and Grosie moved into the brownstone house with her bridegroom, his parents, and his sisters, Margaret, Lizzie, Tilly, and Hanna. Although the Mollers' New York residence was large enough to become, eventually, the headquarters of the Women's National Republican Club, Grosie found the house cramped, in comparison with her family's mansion in Oakland.

If John's Billy had known Grosie as well then as he did later, I guess he would have started packing his bags. At any rate, her health started to decline, and she didn't really perk up until her doctor suggested that perhaps what she needed was a permanent change in climate. I don't mean to imply that her illness was affected. At one time she was really desperately sick, and lost her first baby. But the point is that, one way or another, she convinced John's Billy of the wisdom of moving West.

Old Frederick Delger, glad to have his daughter back home again, rewarded his son-in-law by helping him buy a partnership in a wholesale and retail hardware business in Oakland and San Francisco. And now that they were living on the West Coast, where there weren't such a confusing number of cousins named William, Grosie changed her husband's nickname from John's Billy to Willie.

They built a comfortable house near the Delger mansion. Although Grosie quickly regained a measure of her health, she was never altogether vigorous again. And Papa (as his children and we grandchildren called him) always treated her like a fragile invalid. Actually, she bore him nine splendid children, and outlived him by seven years. She was seventy-six when she died in 1930.

Papa was a sharp businessman, and although old Delger helped him at first, he soon became wealthy in his own right. By the time he was fifty, he had built a mansion of his own for his growing family. The Oakland paper said that the Mollers' place was even more "elegant" than the Delgers', and that its stables could not be "excelled for hygienic advantages." It only had one elevator, though, and apparently no grottoes at all.

When Papa first arrived in California, he didn't know a soul except the Delgers. So perhaps it was natural that after Lillie was born he spent a great deal of time with her. As his oldest daughter, she helped him look after Grosie, especially during her confinements. Papa called Lillie his Little Firefly, partly because of her reddish blonde hair and partly because she moved so quickly.

Every time Grosie left the premises, Papa worried about her, and didn't relax until she was safely back home. One of the first things Lillie remembered was holding Papa's hand while he paced the floor nervously, waiting for Grosie to return from some tea party. Firefly quickly grasped this anxiety about Grosie's health, and then magnified it all out of proportion.

Whereas Papa only feared that Grosie might overexert herself, Firefly thought that he was keeping the truth from her, and that her mother was about to die. Sometimes during Grosie's absences, the little girl would burst into tears, certain that her mother was already dead.

Also, when Grosie took an afternoon nap, Firefly would sit in the garden and weep, convinced that her mother was going to die in her sleep. Only when she saw her mother raise her windowshade, at the end of the nap, did she dry her eyes.

This concern about Grosie's health caused Lillie to take over quite early some of the responsibilities of rearing her younger brothers and sisters.

It was about this time, too, that a thoughtless nurse implanted in her mind the idea that she was an ugly duckling compared to her younger sisters, and especially to a slightly older and quite handsome cousin, Annie Florence Brown.

Without meaning to, Grandma Delger may also have contributed to Lillie's feeling of inferiority, for the hearty old woman never could understand the teary-eyed and mouselike demeanor of the oldest Moller grandchild.

Almost every day, Grandma Delger would come rolling up to the Mollers' gate, driving her own phaeton and wrapped snugly in a robe. The floor of the four-wheeler would be piled high with vegetables from the Delger place, and as she handed them to the Mollers' stableboy, she'd tease Lillie.

"Ach, vot a pale liddle girl. Vy don't you play in der yard

and get some color in der face? Dot's all now. Grandma got to go. Ja! Giddap, Ruthie."

Lillie knew that her grandmother always brought a bag of ladyfingers for the Moller children, and that the bag was hidden under the robe. But she was too bashful to ask for the present, and this sometimes irritated the old lady.

"Ja, Grandma got to go," she'd repeat. "Giddap, Ruthie." She'd hold the reins tight, so that Ruthie couldn't go, despite her order. When Lillie remained silent, the old woman would shake her head, probe under the blanket for the package, and hand it to the girl.

"Ja, dot's der quiet one," she would complain. "Now dis time, Ruthie, when I say giddap I mean giddap."

When Firefly reached the age of six and it was time to send her to school, she simply couldn't face up to going. And since neither Grosie nor Papa could bear to make her unhappy, she was given a one-year reprieve.

"But remember, Lillie-dear," Grosie told her, "I'm afraid you're going to *have* to go next year. But, meanwhile, I'll tutor you at home."

"By next year, I won't mind going at all—not when I'm seven," Lillie fibbed hopefully.

When the next year came, though, Lillie still couldn't make herself go, and Grosie and Papa still couldn't bring themselves to lay down the law.

So it wasn't until Lillie was eight—and should have been in the third grade—that her parents decided to be firm.

"You know as well as I do, dear," said Grosie, "that this year we simply *must* send you."

"I know," sobbed the little girl. "I'll try to go. I promise I'll try. But I don't know whether I can."

"All you can do, honey," Papa comforted his Firefly, "is to *try*. No one can ask any more than that."

Grosie took her, about a week later, to a private school for girls, named Snell's Seminary. Of course she was the "new girl." The others in the class giggled and mocked her, partly because she was new and partly because they had heard from their mothers that the Moller girl was a shy little thing who was afraid to come to school, and who was such a mama's darling—not to mention papa's—that they wouldn't send her.

Lillie entered the classroom dry-eyed, looking straight ahead. When the teacher assigned a desk to her, she sat down at it, folded her hands tightly, placed them carefully on the surface, and stared at them.

She vowed she wouldn't cry until she got home.

When the teacher finally called on her to recite, her lips trembled, and she couldn't talk above a whisper.

"We can't hear you, Lillie," said the teacher.

The little girl tried again, but still no more than a whisper emerged.

"For goodness' sake, speak up!" the teacher demanded impatiently.

"I can't," she whispered miserably.

"You can, too! We're not going to eat her, are we children?"

The children giggled and smacked their lips, as if eating her was exactly what they had in mind.

Lillie stared woodenly at her hands.

"Then just sit there all day looking at your desk, and I'll call on somebody else," snapped the teacher.

The children tittered again, but Lillie told herself they'd never see her cry, and they didn't.

At recess, she ducked through a hedge and ran all the way home, where she cried so uncontrollably that Papa had to send for a doctor, who put her to bed for a few days. So Grosie and Papa decided to keep her out of school for still another year.

Naturally, that suited Lillie. And in later years, some of her most pleasant memories revolved around tutoring sessions with her mother, on a green bench under a linden tree in their garden.

"I came to know every tree, bush and plant," Lillie subsequently wrote. "How well I remember the palm tree and the formal beds of tiny flowers that circled it; the pepper tree and its rose-colored berries; the eucalyptus tree with its tall trunk and look of distant places. Just the names of the flowers in my mother's garden bring back happy memories: sweet briar, lemon verbena, lavender heliotrope, breath-of-heaven, mignonette. They remind me of my mother and of beauty and serenity."

Firefly's favorite retreat within the house was a nook behind the draperies in the parlor. She'd lie on her stomach there, on a few cushions, and read endlessly by the light which rainbowed through a stained-glass window. Sometimes she'd become so engrossed she wouldn't hear her mother when she was called to meals. And her mother would have to come through the draperies to get her.

"I *do* wish you'd answer," Grosie would tell her in about as firm a tone as she ever used.

"I'll try to hear you better after this, Mama-dear," Lillie would reply.

The next autumn, when she was nine, Lillie still couldn't make herself return to the girls' school. She finally did agree, though, to go to public school.

The principal, aghast at the thought of a child's being tutored at home, insisted on putting her in the first grade, along with tots who couldn't read, whereas she was already reading everything in sight and had practically memorized the complete and unabridged works of Louisa May Alcott.

Being the big girl in a class of tots resulted in some ridicule, too, but in many ways it helped bridge the gap between home and school. By that time Lillie had five younger sisters, and was accustomed to helping them. And she soon found that she was a sort of assistant teacher in the first grade. Then, as soon as she adjusted to school life, she was allowed to skip grades and catch up with her age group. But she still suffered occasionally from what her mother called "Monday morning headaches."

She quickly became an excellent student, and inevitably was accused of being a teacher's pet.

"Maybe that's just what I was, too," she once wrote. "You see, I decided that since I couldn't be pretty, I *had* to be smart."

She considered herself so unattractive that she'd cross the street to avoid talking to a boy. Once she received a comic valentine, and ran home again in tears, sure she had been singled out because she was homely.

Yet pictures of her as a young schoolgirl are certainly pretty enough—every bit as pretty as the sisters and cousins she imagined to be so much more attractive than she.

As she advanced into high school, she wouldn't believe her father when he kept telling her she was "a real little belle." She thought he was either prejudiced or trying to make her forget that she was so terribly plain.

Even when boys started paying attention to her, she thought they probably wanted help with their algebra or Latin homework. Sometimes, when boys sat next to her on the horsecar going home from school, she actually *would* help them with their studies.

Bit by bit, though, she managed to conquer some of her shyness, especially among her girl classmates, many of whom remained her close friends for the rest of their lives.

During her senior year, she made straight A's, and exhibited some talent as a budding poet, in contributions to the school paper, *The Aegis*. Meanwhile, she also was studying music with a gifted Oakland composer named John Metcalfe. He thought she had real ability as a musician, and he admired her poetry so much that he asked her to write lyrics to several melodies. One song they collaborated on, called "Sunrise," was played in the high school.

But then, just when she started to feel that she was being accepted as "one of the crowd," an incident occurred that put her, at least temporarily, back in her shell. She used to tell us children about the incident, to point up the moral that occasionally Mother-knows-best.

"I remember that when I was a child," she'd say, "I was like you—I sometimes thought I knew more than my mother did. So a few weeks before I graduated from high school, I told her that all the senior girls had decided to wear figured dimity dresses to commencement, instead of formal white.

" 'Why, Lillie-dear, I never heard of such a thing!' my mother insisted. 'I know those girls and I know their mothers. And I'm sure that, in the end, they'll wear white.'

" 'No, Mama-dear,' I told her, 'they're going to wear figured dimity. You wouldn't want me to be the only girl in the class in white, would you?'

" 'No,' said Mama, 'but even worse would be for all of them to be in white, and for you to be in figured dimity. And I fear that's just what's going to happen—that the other girls will decide at the last minute to wear white.'

" 'Oh, no they won't,' I assured her. 'We've all promised, Mama-dear.'

"So I wore a figured dimity to commencement. And every single other girl in the class wore white. Well, we all sat up there on the stage, and I was never so embarrassed *in my life!* And you couldn't blame my mother for pointing out that she had told me so, could you?"

She could laugh about it then, all right. But at the time she felt that some of the girls she had counted on as friends had all but deliberately teamed up against her. Choking back tears, she had sat there on the stage, a conspicuous blob of color in a sea of billowing white gauze.

Later that day, at a party her family gave for her, the dessert was homemade strawberry ice cream. The strawberries were frozen hard as rocks, and one impolite male guest proved to be the life of the party by calling attention repeatedly to this unfortunate circumstance. He'd place a strawberry between his teeth, position his chin on the edge of the dining room table, and then thump the top of his head, sledgehammer-fashion, with his fist. Everyone laughed, but in the Mollers' well-regulated household, neither the frozen strawberries nor the breach of etiquette on the part of the would-be masticator was deemed hilarious.

In later years, when Lillie had disciplined herself to the point where she could almost erase unpleasantries as if they had never occurred, she doubtless could have found something cheerful to write, as her graduation day came to a close. Perhaps she might have written something like, "Although I didn't plan it that way, I was certainly the center of all eyes in the lovely dimity dress my mother had had specially made for me. Then we had my favorite dessert, strawberry ice cream, and the ice cream itself was delicious even though the strawberries were frozen."

But in actual fact, when the party was over Lillie went to her room and wrote on her commencement program, "The end of a dreadful day!"

CHAPTER 3

Ruffles but No Flourishes

During her last year in high school, Lillie made a thorough study of the situation, and decided she was doomed to spinsterhood.

The study was composed of a number of brief but critical inspections, in the mirror of the bedroom which she shared with her youngest sister, Josephine. The mirror on the wall told her, in what stands as a monumental error in prognosticating, that she'd never have any children of her own, for the simple reason that she was too plain to attract and marry the sort of man who would make her happy.

Actually, Josephine was more like a daughter to Lillie than a sister. After six California-born girls, Grosie had just given birth to the first of three Moller sons. Needing some assistance in looking after two-year-old Josephine, Grosie had called Lillie to her bedside and said:

"I'm going to give Josephine to you, Lillie-dear, to help bring up. You will have a crib next to your bed, for your little sister. Will you like that?"

Any girl who enjoyed leaping out of bed at the crack of dawn every morning to pick a bouquet for her mother's breakfast tray, could be counted upon to enjoy a baby sister as a roommate, I suppose. Anyway, Lillie told her mother that she would enjoy a great deal having Jo as her living-doll and crib-fellow.

Far from getting on each other's nerves, the two sisters never considered the bedroom they shared to be overpopulated. Even in later years, Lillie always thought of Jo as her favorite sister, and in fact the "smartest, prettiest, and most attractive" of the Moller girls.

As for Jo, she once confided that "when Lillie told us to do something, we just naturally *wanted* to do it. She was so good to us that we wouldn't have done anything to make her unhappy."

That was Lillie's technique, all right, learned firsthand from Grosie, the past-master. I can vouch for the fact that the technique is more effective when it comes to keeping order than threats of the whipping post and Chinese water torture, employed on occasion by my father.

At any rate, after Lillie agreed to be Josephine's second mother, they moved into the tower room of the Mollers' Victorian house, where Lillie had her own closet, washstand, bookcases, and worktable. It was in the privacy of the tower that she decided she might as well reconcile herself to being a bachelor girl.

She was determined to *contribute* to society, even if she couldn't participate in the population growth—to be productive if not reproductive. So she decided she should have a career, either in music or teaching.

Her music teacher, Mr. Metcalfe, thought she was talented enough to have a successful career in music, provided she was willing to devote full time to her work. Some of her high school teachers, on the other hand, urged her to go to college.

It was still somewhat unusual in those days for a girl to attend college. Grosie and Papa felt that it was both a waste of time and vaguely unladylike.

"College may be useful for a woman who knows she may have to earn her own living," Papa kept telling his Firefly. "But no daughter of mine will ever have to do that!"

This turned out to be another fairly spectacular error in prognosticating, because twenty-eight years later Lillie was confronted with a situation wherein she not only had to make a living for herself, but also had our thundering herd to feed.

But even as Grosie and Papa were repeating that college wasn't advisable for a girl, they realized that times were changing—and their own viewpoint was gradually weakening. Instrumental in helping them change their minds was Lillie's vivacious cousin, Annie Florence, who had entered the University of California two years before. No one could accuse Annie Flo of being unladylike, even if she *was* something pretty close to a Gay Nineties version of Betty Coed. Grosie and Papa thought a lot of her, and were inclined to excuse the fact that she was so active in campus dramatics and other activities that she was forever getting her name in the newspapers.

Grosie was the first to throw in the sponge, and then Papa followed suit. "All right, Lillie," he surrendered, "go ahead and try college for a year, then. But for goodness' sake try to keep your name out of the papers."

So Lillie gave up her music lessons and the thought of

being a musician. And with Annie Flo lending a helping hand, she registered as a freshman at the university in the autumn of 1896.

Lillie didn't live on the campus. Her parents wouldn't have allowed it and besides she preferred to stay at home. She was asked to join several sororities, but Papa didn't allow that, either. She was perfectly content to ride the streetcar to and from the campus every day, to help her mother bring up Jo and the other children, and to spend pleasant hours every evening over her books.

She majored in literature, so that she could eventually become an English teacher, and also devoted a good deal of time to philosophy and modern languages. She took almost no science or mathematics, both of which would have been useful to her later.

For a while, Papa kept grumbling around the house that college was no place for one of his daughters. But he finally was silenced by a long-time friend, Professor Putzka, who taught at the university. Putzka came to the Mollers' house regularly, on Thursday nights, to play billiards with Papa. And he finally got tired of the grumbling.

"Look, Moller, this is California, not Germany of two generations ago," he scolded. "You talk as if no girl had ever gone to college before. Miss Lillie is one of the best students in the whole freshman class, and she has a mind that should be given the best opportunities."

Lillie also followed Annie Flo's footsteps in campus dramatics, and was chosen for an important part in the Charter Day play—an annual affair observing the founding of the university. Although she dreaded the opening-night performance, she found like many another tyro that her nervousness disappeared shortly after the curtain went up—and that she thoroughly enjoyed herself.

The only trouble was that she gave such a good performance she *did* get her name in the paper.

"I *knew* it," said Papa, thumping the Oakland newspaper. "Not yet twenty years old, and already her name is plastered all over the metropolitan press."

Lillie pointed out that the Oakland newspapers were hardly the metropolitan press, and that the mere mention of her name in the body of a story hardly constituted a real plastering.

"But you don't understand, Lillie-dear," Grossie put in. "A lady's name should appear only three times in the newspaper—when she's born . . ."

"I know, Mama-dear," sighed Lillie, patiently finishing the cliché. "But if the poor thing doesn't marry, she only gets two write-ups. So maybe my name will only be in the paper three times, after all."

"Don't you worry about *that*, dear," Grosie smiled. "When the right man comes along—well, we'll see."

"Mr. Right," said Lillie, rolling her eyes and teasing her mother with an exaggeratedly romantic sigh, "may I introduce Miss Wrong."

"We'll see," Grosie repeated. "Just you wait!"

"And, anyway," chuckled Papa, "how could *anybody* maintain that a world-famous actress was Miss Wrong?"

Thereafter, Lillie's name was in the paper fairly often, because she appeared in a good many campus plays, and her parents became reconciled to—and perhaps even a little proud of—her publicity. She gained poise with each performance, and they *do* say that she practically had them in the aisles, during her senior year, when she played the bewigged Baronne de Vaubert, in *Mademoiselle de la Zieglière*.

Among the professors she remembered best were Charles Mills Gayley, a Dubliner who taught Shakespeare and whom she once described as "simply a spellbinder—so much so that hundreds of San Francisco and Oakland girls tried to crash his classes"; Louis Syle of the drama department, who was a close friend of many great actors of the day; and George Stratton, a young man who was teaching the relatively new subject of psychology.

The record indicates that, except for participating in dramatics, she was a dead-serious student. Yet I can vouch for the fact that—at least vicariously—she was somewhat of a rah-rah girl, too, because certainly she knew all of the college cheers.

I remember once, when I was quite young, watching with wide-eyed incredulity when Lillie departed from her dignified demeanor long enough to show us, with a vicious swing of an imaginary tomahawk, just what the Golden Bears proposed to do to the Stanford Indians, back when *she* was a girl.

I have forgotten just what triggered the demonstration. Perhaps one of my older sisters was discussing the cheerleading at Montclair High School. But Mother suddenly dropped to one knee and started her fists going in circles like the treadmills in Aunt Lillian's squirrel cages. Then, making a swooping leap and swinging that tomahawk like billy-be-damned, she started to bellow in a fierce, gravelly voice utterly different from her usually modulated tones:

"Give 'em the axe, the axe, the axe! Where? Right in the neck, the neck, the neck . . ."

So, dead-serious or not, she obviously found time to keep up with the prowess of the university's athletic heroes.

Her own biggest triumph came during the spring of her senior year when the university's president, Dr. Benjamin Ide Wheeler, summoned her to his ivory tower and informed her she had been named a speaker for Commencement Day.

Dr. Wheeler was a gentle soul who wouldn't have hurt

anyone's feelings for the world. But he had a message he wanted to get across to Lillie, and, bless his soul, he couldn't quite figure how to tackle the subject.

The message was that, while he believed wholeheartedly in coeducation, he had no use for those feminists who affected mannish haircuts and attire. And he wanted to be sure that, even though Lillie would be wearing a graduation gown, she'd look and act like a woman.

"You know, Miss Moller," he said, carefully edging into the subject, "we never have had a woman on the program before, and the faculty and I decided we would like to have you be the one to set the precedent."

Lillie said she was simply overwhelmed.

"Congratulations, Miss Moller."

Lillie thanked him, and rose to go. But he asked her to stay for a minute, and then cleared his throat.

"When you deliver your speech . . . ," he said, and then drew up lamely to a stop.

"Yes," Lillie encouraged him.

". . . my advice is," he finally blurted out, "to wear a dress with *ruffles*—ruffles that will show at the top of your graduation gown."

Lillie took out her notebook and noncommittally jotted down, "dress with ruffles."

Having passed this first hurdle, Dr. Wheeler was emboldened to speak his whole piece. "*Please* don't give an oration," he continued. "People don't like women to give orations. And Miss Moller, this is important: Don't make a lot of bombastic gestures; and don't scream!"

"Ruffles without flourishes," wrote Lillie. "No screaming."

"And one more thing: Read what you have to say, and from small pieces of paper. Don't imitate a man. Look and speak like a woman."

It was good advice, and Lillie followed it right down to the last ruffle. The graduation ceremonies were held in the university's new gymnasium. The Oakland newspaper reported with typical California modesty that, although the gym was perhaps the largest in the country, it was still "too small for the thousands who sought entrance."

Lillie was terribly nervous when she was first called forward. She found it was a good deal more nerve-racking to appear as herself on the stage than as a character in a play. But once again, her stage fright departed when she started to talk.

White ruffles blossomed plentifully from her black graduation gown. Her subject was a typical one for a commencement: *Life—a Means or an End?*

Her parents and all of her sisters were in the audience. Dr. Brown, the family minister, whispered in Papa's ear that Lillie "ought to be in the pulpit taking my place."

The next day both the Oakland and San Francisco papers contained not only her name but her picture, and one of the San Francisco write-ups even went so far as to say that "Miss Moller made the most interesting speech of the day."

Papa was now so proud of his Firefly that he clipped out the articles and sent them to his family in New York. It took Grosie a little longer to adjust to the situation, but finally she told Lillie:

"If your picture *had* to be in the papers, Lillie-dear, I'm glad it was in such a dignified manner."

"With ruffles," smiled Lillie.

That summer, Lillie managed somehow to convince her family she should study for a master's degree in English at Columbia University in New York. Professor Putzka, Papa's billiard-playing friend, again was instrumental in helping her get her way. Of course, as Lillie well knew when she first broached the subject, Papa would never even have considered it if it weren't for the fact that his sisters were still living in New York and could keep an eye on her.

Grosie insisted that her permission hinged on Lillie's buying a whole new wardrobe. Most women of twenty-two would have liked nothing better, but to Lillie buying clothes was just another chore. It wasn't that she didn't appreciate nice things—it was rather that, to her, a thing didn't have to be new to be nice. And she was well pleased with the clothes she was already wearing.

Just the same, she complied with her mother's wishes, and bought the new wardrobe.

When it came to shopping, Lillie thought the most painful experience was going to a fashionable milliner, patronized by all the Moller and Delger women, and sitting around self-consciously while fluttering females draped grapes, feathers, flowers, and other artificial flora and fauna over the bare shell of hats they were designing for her.

"Now try *this* one, Miss Moller," the milliner kept repeating. "Isn't it precious!" Then as Lillie apologetically plunked the hat on the top of her head, the milliner would scold her, "No, not *that* way, Miss Moller. *Please,* not that way. You have it on backwards!"

Finally, with her hats in boxes and her dresses in a steamer trunk, Lillie journeyed to New York and obtained a room in a dormitory at Barnard College, the women's branch of Columbia University.

Like Grosie, Lillie was so homesick in New York that it actually affected her physically, and the climate didn't agree with her either. Although Papa's sisters did their best to make her feel at home, she longed for her family and the West Coast.

To make matters worse, she had wanted particularly to attend the classes and brilliant lectures of James Brander Matthews, the writer-educator-critic, but discovered that he wouldn't teach women. Even when Matthews got the word that Miss Moller had come all the way from California—and had chosen Barnard—because of his courses, he stood firm.

"And I don't care if she *did* make the commencement speech out there," he is reported to have snorted to his dean. "She is *not* going to distract my classes or me. I'm still old-fashioned enough to believe that a woman's place is in the home."

It wasn't the first time—and it wouldn't be the last—that Lillie got the word about where her place was.

Although Lillie believed in women's rights with all her heart, she believed just as strongly that no lady should make a spectacle of herself. And, anyway, the last thing in the world she would do would be to force herself into a class where she wasn't wanted. So she didn't press the issue, and instead arranged a schedule with professors who weren't prejudiced against "co-education"—a word that was just beginning to come into the language.

In November, when winter started to move into New York, she came down with a series of colds and then with an acute case of pleurisy and an alarmingly high fever. A university official notified the Moller aunts, who quickly arrived at her dormitory in a carriage heaped high with hot water bottles and quilts, and whisked Lillie off to their house.

Then they telegraphed Papa that she was sick. And the next day, when they had discovered that she was not only sick but miserable and unhappy, they telegraphed him again that he'd better come East and take his daughter back home.

And Lillie felt a little as if she hadn't been able to meet the challenge—just as she hadn't been able to meet it when she was a child and had run away from Snell's Seminary.

Remembering how Grosie had almost died in New York, Papa came East on the next train. By then, he had become such a thoroughly converted Californian he was convinced the New York weather was enough to kill anyone. So he sent Lillie telegrams, from various stops en route, urging her to keep bundled up until he could get her back to God's Country and the Great Open Spaces.

By the time he arrived in New York, Lillie's fever was down, and she was packed and ready to go. Papa kept assuring his sisters that she would regain her strength quickly, back in God's Country—a cliché which, although they were extremely fond of him, they were finding increasingly difficult to endure. But the fact is that he was entirely correct, and Lillie was as strong as ever within a week after their return to Oakland.

She spent the next ten months luxuriating around the house, reading, and helping her mother with the children. Then she went back to her alma mater—still living at home —to study for her master's.

She chose for her thesis Ben Jonson's *Bartholomew Fair,* a comedy satirizing the Puritans, and memorized page after page of his poetry, which, subsequently, she used to enjoy reciting to us, sometimes with purposely overdramatic gestures. One of her favorites went:

> Underneath this sable hearse
> Lies the subject of all verse—
> Sidney's sister, Pembroke's mother.
> Death, ere thou hast slain another
> Learn'd and fair and good as she
> Time shall throw a dart at thee.

As she became more and more engrossed in the early seventeenth century, she paid, if anything, even less attention to the clothes styles of the day. And after she received her master's degree in 1902, she didn't change her ways.

Grosie finally became fairly reconciled to this, but it was a real thorn in the flesh of the milliner. On one occasion, as Lillie walked along a street in downtown Oakland, she heard an indignant, nasal whinny which she recognized as belonging to the milliner.

"Miss Moller, *please!*" implored the milliner. "You're going to ruin my business."

Lillie sheepishly reached up and reversed her hat. "Is that better now?" she asked brightly.

"You're going to ruin me," choked the milliner, on the verge of tears.

"I'm terribly sorry," Lillie apologized. "Really I am. It's not that I'm absentminded. It's simply that I can't tell the front from the back."

The milliner took her firmly by the arm, and led her across the street to the hat shop. "Just have a seat, Miss Moller," she said icily.

Lillie sat down, and the exasperated woman stitched a white X at the front of the inside band.

"So the X always goes at the front," said Lillie, trying to make some light conversation. "That's easy to remember. Why didn't we think of that before?"

"At the front," conceded the milliner through pursed lips.

"There," said Lillie triumphantly, clapping the hat on her head with the X in front, but without bothering to face a mirror. "Is that better?"

"Ye gads!" sighed the milliner. "Yes, I guess it's better, Miss Moller. But not very *much* better."

I wish I could report that, through the years, Lillie became more hat-conscious—but unfortunately that wasn't the case. Some fifty-five years later, when she was on the West Coast for the wedding of one of her grandsons, she found she needed a hat, and went into the nearest hat store.

After looking over the wares on a counter for less than a minute, she picked up a little number, put it on her head, and asked the sales girl if she thought it would do.

"I guess it's all right," said the girl, "but you have it on backwards."

In all fairness, I ought to add that my sister Anne, who was there at the time, goes on to say that at the wedding itself Mother was impeccably dressed, had her hat on right-side-to, and "looked beautiful."

CHAPTER 4

Bunker Oats Are Free

Martha Bunker, a stern and rockbound female who was to become Lillie's mother-in-law, was born in the village of North Anson, Maine, August 26, 1834.

While blunt and utterly devoid of tact, Martha was nevertheless generous, warmhearted, intelligent, industrious, and honest. Sometimes she was a good deal too honest, because she'd tell you exactly what she thought. She was the sort of New Englander who, if asked whether she didn't think a third party was looking mighty pretty today, felt called upon to squint her eyes in appraisal, walk slowly around the third party, and then give a considered, accurate, and painfully candid answer—which might include recommendations to stop slouching and have an unsightly mole removed.

More than anyone except Lillie herself, Martha shaped the life of her son. She also, to a lesser extent, shaped Lillie's. The time came, eventually, when Lillie thought of her as a second mother.

"The longer I live, the more I realize what a fine, good, kind person she was," Lillie once wrote. "She was the best of New England."

But for the first few years of her married life, Lillie was both overawed by and sometimes downright scared silly of her outspoken mother-in-law.

As part of her marriage agreement, Lillie accepted not only Martha, for better or worse, but also Martha's old-maid sister, a talented but irascible artist named Caroline. Kit, as this sister was usually called, was just as blunt as Martha, but not so warmhearted.

No one ever lived who had a greater respect for education than Martha. She had been a schoolteacher as a young woman, and she thought that the first duty of every parent was to see that his children had all the schooling they were mentally able to absorb. She taught my older sisters and me how to read and write even before we went to kindergarten, and later checked our lessons at night to be sure we were making proper headway.

One of the things I liked best about my grandmother was that, if I had a nightmare, she allowed me to crawl into her bed. Since she didn't believe in playing favorites, she also extended bed privileges to all my brothers and sisters. So sometimes there were four or five little creatures snuggled around her when she awoke in the morning.

But if all of us could sometimes have our own way with Grandma, others were not so fortunate in dealing with her —particularly the domestic help. She addressed most of them by their surnames, without benefit of a Mr. or Mrs. She felt that part of her mission in life was to elevate the morals, sanitation, and energy of Irish immigrants. And since our domestics were Irish, she had periodic discussions with them about such matters as the necessity for frequent baths, the merits of prompt rising in the morning, and the dire dangers of breaking biblical admonitions dealing with theft, truthfulness, and coveting one's neighbor's ass.

Even when she was pushing eighty, she always laundered all her own underwear—and hung it in the yard on the handyman's afternoon off—rather than to place any "temptations in his lecherous hands."

Strong as an ox, self-sufficient, portly, and the possessor of a generous prow, an ample stern, and an even keel, Martha traced her lineage back to William Bradford, Pilgrim father and governor of the Plymouth Colony.

Her father, Daniel (Bull) Bunker, was said to be one of the strongest men in the State of Maine. He was born in Vienna, Maine, September 23, 1799, raised a family of fifteen children, and lived to be eighty-four.

Daniel was a sixth-generation descendant of James Bunker (sometimes Buckner), who was baptized in Slapton, Devonshire, England, February 10, 1633, and first appears in Kittery, Maine, in 1646. James subsequently moved to nearby Dover, New Hampshire, and the thousands of American Bunkers who descend from him are known as the Dover branch of the clan.

Daniel earned his nickname by throwing and breaking the neck of an enraged dairy bull which had knocked down and was trampling a woman at a husking bee.

Bull was blue-eyed, ruddy-faced, sandy-haired, and big-headed—traits which were passed along to my father and to some of the present generation. Like many a farmer of his day, he had a battle-royal with the railroad when workmen tried to lay tracks through his best field. In traditional fashion, Bull drove off the railroad men with a needle-sharp pitchfork. Since he had served two terms as sheriff, not to mention twenty-five years as deputy sheriff, no law officer could be found who was willing to serve a legal condemnation notice on *any* of the Bunker clan—let alone on Big Bull personally. So eventually the railroad decided to curve its tracks slightly, and go through the property of a less belligerent neighbor, who had fewer kinfolk and never had been sheriff.

Daniel was a pillar of his church and school system, and a clipping from the Fairfield, Maine, newspaper—where he ran a "temperance hotel" in his later years—says he also was "the means of making a free bridge of the toll bridge between this village and Benton, after other efforts had failed." Whether this also was accomplished with the aid of a pitchfork isn't spelled out.

It's easy to see where his daughter, Martha, obtained her vast respect for education, because Daniel himself put "schoolin' " at the very top of his list of necessities for his children.

He moved from a rural log house into the village of North Anson in 1830, when his oldest child reached school age. With his own hands, he built a large house in North Anson, for his growing brood. Martha remembered being carried piggyback through snowdrifts to school by her father, when she was four years old.

A few years later, he talked the village fathers into building a new school. But money and enthusiasm ran out before the building was completed, and Daniel then finished the work all by himself.

"He was never reimbursed, and no man in town was less able to afford the time and money to do it," Martha subsequently wrote.

The Bunkers kept a small flock of sheep, and used the wool to make clothes, blankets, and rugs. Daniel made the shoes by hand from cowhide.

When she was middle-aged, Martha jotted down some reminiscences of her girlhood. She was a good student, she wrote, but wasn't very popular with boys because, "I had a red streak in my hair, which was considered a crime."

One entry tells of being invited to her first dance:

"An old friend of the family had sent us a bottle of choice bear's oil from Moose Head Lake. I soaked my hair with the oil until it dripped, thus subduing the red. When the little boy called for me, he crooked his elbow, and I caught onto it bravely enough, like the older girls. I let go of it, as we approached the hall, where people might see me. And toward the last I left him altogether and walked along the other side of the road."

Martha wrote that all the children in North Anson wore camphor bags around their necks, dangling from red string, to ward off diseases. The adults wore gold beads to ward off scrofula. The heart of a hot onion was the cure for earaches.

The Bunkers were "poor but proud"—but not as much so as one family of nine boys. They didn't have enough shoes to go around, so when they went to church they'd go in two groups—and the first group would secretly drop its shoes out of the window, so the second group could also walk into the building properly shod and with heads held high. When church was over, they'd all wait until everyone else had gone before they departed.

In 1849, when gold was discovered in California, "Everyone took out maps to see just where California was," Martha wrote. "There was a lot of talk about all the Indian country you had to pass through; and of being scalped; and about the alternatives of going overland through Panama or around Cape Horn. Many who left town were never heard from again."

All nine of the boys from the poor family—some still

shoeless—set out for California in a covered wagon pulled by oxen—and all struck it rich. Then they returned, with their pockets full of money, to North Anson, and the whole town turned out to greet them. Later, they all went back to California, "taking with them girls of their youth as brides."

Visiting ministers, lecturers, phrenologists, and "daguerreotype artists" who passed through town were always welcome at the Bunkers' house, and of course their horses were stabled in Daniel's barn. Soon the word spread over much of the state that "Bunker Oats Are Free"—an expression which Grandma sometimes employed in later years when she thought that deadbeats were imposing on us.

"My father invited one phrenologist to stay at our house," Martha wrote, "and he spent several evenings examining our heads. He gave everyone a fairly good character except me. He said I was a heedless, careless girl. Then all members of the family looked at each other as much as to say, 'He surely knows his business!'

"But then he added, to make peace all around, that I might raise a President of the United States.

"When a daguerreotype artist took our pictures, my father placed them in a large frame. Each of us, as he grew older and in his judgment better looking, destroyed his old picture—saying he couldn't bear to think he had ever looked like *that*—whenever a new one was taken."

Martha was only fifteen years old when she obtained a job as schoolteacher, in a country community not far from North Anson, where some of the children were literally sewn into their clothes for the winter months.

She moved into a boarding house, and they took special pains to favor her, since she was the schoolmarm. For instance, she always got the biggest piece of pie—even if the lady of the house *did* lick the knife "at every cut."

Although she tried to act assured and mature, Martha was terribly homesick and spent many a night alone in her room, weeping silently into her pillow. But it never even occurred to her to give up and go home.

There were twenty or so children in the one-room school, and six or seven of them were older than the new schoolmarm.

Martha said the superintendent took her to the schoolhouse and introduced her. Then he asked one of the older boys to draw a diagram of the desks and list the names of the children, so she'd know where everyone sat.

"They were all on their best behavior when he was there," Martha said, "but as soon as he left they started to cut the fool. When I turned my back I heard some moving, and when I faced the class again I was pretty sure some of them had swapped seats.

"After that, when I called Tom, Jim would answer, and so forth—and the whole class would titter. I felt like bawling and running out of the place. But I didn't let them know it. So I bit the bullet instead, and stood in front of them with the seating chart in one hand and a ruler in the other."

The fifteen-year-old schoolmarm asked them sternly whether everyone was in his correct seat. Practically in unison, they assured her insolently that, yes, ma'am, Miss Bunker, everyone surely was. Miss Bunker stalked up to the desk of the biggest boy in the class, a six-footer with half an inch of beard.

"You, boy," she said, consulting the seating chart, "are Tom Pierce?"

"Yes, ma'am," he smirked.

"Back in North Anson where I come from," Martha told him, "we have an expression about being too stupid to know your own name. You go home and fetch your father. Tell him the new schoolmarm says she can teach most anybody, but not boys who don't know their names." She stretched to her full five feet four inches and brought the ruler down on his desk with a menacing whack. "Now git!"

The boy managed a grin for the rest of the class, and departed. But a couple of minutes later he reappeared, shamefacedly minus the grin.

"Please, ma'am," he said, "I've remembered my name. It ain't Tom Pierce, it's Jim Hardy."

"Now that's better, boy," Martha conceded. "But I told you to fetch your father."

"If I do," Jim blurted out, "he'll lick me."

"And if you don't," said the fifteen-year-old schoolmarm, jutting out her chin, "*I'll* lick you."

"Please, Miss Bunker," said Jim, sighing with relief, "if I get to do the choosin', I'll take one of *your* lickings."

"Will you write me a list of everyone who changed seats?"

Jim started for the door, and Martha asked him where he was going.

"Home to get my licking."

"Never mind, boy. Come in here and sit down. I can't tolerate a tattle-tale-tit any more than you can."

She turned her back to the class and walked to the front of the room. Behind her, she heard the floorboards creak, as the children tiptoed to their right seats.

"What I learned that first day of teaching always stood me in good stead," Martha wrote. "If you don't show children that you propose to train them, they'll end up training you.

"My schoolhouse was full of children, and I thought I was expected to fit every one of them for college. So I worked hard, and even though I was only fifteen, I never did better work."

She was paid a dollar twenty-five a week, which was the usual rate in Maine. After ten weeks, she "took account of the things I longed for," and bought a white muslin dress and a black silk cape, known as a visite.

Most of Martha's brothers and sisters eventually migrated, because opportunities in Maine were so limited. I can't call the roll of all of them. But Bainbridge, who was nineteen, died at sea en route to the California gold mines. The Bunkers received a letter from one of Bainbridge's boyhood friends saying, "We wrapped him in a blanket and lowered him down. I took charge of his things and sold what I could. I have his watch and $36.49. Write me what to do with the money. Tell my folks I start for the mines tomorrow morning."

Dan Junior became a prominent citizen of Chicago; Solon was one of the first settlers of Big Piney, Wyoming; Frank and Fred founded Independence, Kansas; Mary became the principal of Science Hill Female Academy at Shelbyville, Kentucky; and Naomi went to California and became a teacher in the Oakland school system—the very system that Lillie Moller attended a generation later.

One brother who stayed in Maine, Benjamin, became a weekly newspaper editor who illustrated his vitriolic articles with even more vitriolic woodcuts which he carved with a jackknife. When he died March 8, 1894, his obituary in a rival weekly (the clipping is pasted in my grandmother's scrapbook, but the name of the paper is unfortunately missing) said with typical down-Maine bluntness:

"It would be difficult finding a man in Maine who has not

heard of Ben Bunker. Possessed as he was of the powers of witty sarcasm and stinging invective, he was a political antagonist whom more feared than loved. Mr. Bunker cared not in the slightest what anyone said or printed in regard to himself. But the man who cast the dart needed to be most securely intrenched, or the unsparing warrior would bring the house down around his ears."

So much for the Tribe of Dan, as the North Anson villagers called Bull Bunker and his fifteen children.

CHAPTER 5

The First Widow Gilbreth

In spite of her reddish hair "which was considered a crime," Martha managed to make one of the best catches of any girl in her part of Maine. His name was John Hiram Gilbreth, and he lived in the nearby town of Fairfield. While still in his early twenties, Hiram—as he was called— was on his way to becoming a rich man, by Maine standards. Besides owning a general store, a stock farm, and some of the best harness horses in New England, he was tall, lean, witty, and good-looking.

Hiram was descended on his mother's side from Governor Thomas Dudley, the Colonial administrator in America, who emigrated to Massachusetts Bay Colony in 1630.

The first Gilbreth ancestor in this country was Patrick Galbraith, a Scot of the clan McDonald. Pat emigrated about 1700 to Vienna, Maine, where he built the first water-powered grain mill in that part of the country. As one Maine historian expressed it, Pat compelled the "lusty vagrant to tread a wheel which should grind corn and wheat for the hard-working settlers." The "lusty vagrant" was, of course, the local stream.

Hiram's father was Benjamin Gilbreth of Belfast, Maine. Sometime between Patrick and Benjamin, the surname was changed from Galbraith to Gilbreth. My father used to say that, about the time of the Revolution, a deaf recorder misspelled the name during the turmoil of an election. The upshot was that the Galbraith of that day would have lost his vote if he hadn't adopted the new name.

Hiram had five brothers and sisters. The most interesting of these, Charles H. Gilbreth, was a mate on a whaling ship and later served under Commodore Matthew Perry in the 1852 mission to open Japan to foreign trade.

Another unidentified clipping in my grandmother's scrapbook says of Charles:

"He was a bold and daring man. . . . On one occasion, on the coast of China, twelve pirates boarded his ship for robbery. He had only six men with him. . . . He seized a sharp sword and descended upon them [the pirates] with the command, 'Up with your hands or off come your heads.' They obeyed, and Charles Gilbreth bound every one of them with cords so that they were at his mercy."

Ah, well! They bred giants in those days.

Martha Bunker was twenty-four and Hiram Gilbreth was twenty-five when they were married in Waterville, Maine, in November 1858. Ten years later, on July 7, 1868, Frank Bunker Gilbreth was born in Fairfield. Two sisters had preceded Frank. The normally dignified Hiram, who always had wanted a son, did a Highland Fling around his parlor.

That same day, Hiram wrote his mother about the good

news, but by then he had regained his New England taciturnity, and was thinking again about his favorite subject, which was how to make money.

"You will be glad to know," he wrote, "that Martha has a nice-looking boy, born this morning at nine o'clock. She is as comfortable as could be expected. Her babe weighs eleven pounds and has dark brown hair. I am in great haste. My business drives me. I have sold twenty-three mowing machines at retail in my store within three days, so you see I am busy."

Although Hiram was proud of his only son, he was just about equally proud of a wonderful Morgan horse he had picked up for a bargain price of $200 two years before.

The horse was a son of the famous trotter General Knox, and Hiram named his horse Gilbreth Knox. I'm not sure how Hiram happened to get the horse so cheaply—perhaps he was a sickly colt. But in any event, Gilbreth Knox ran a total of a hundred and sixty-one races, and won sixty of them. The horse also sired fourteen race-winners. The best of his colts, Lothair, brought $5,000 when he was sold.

As soon as young Frank was old enough to walk, he constantly tagged after his father. Once at Hiram's stock farm, Frank showed that he had firm ideas about having his own way.

In a letter to his sister Abigail, Hiram reported that his three-year-old son grabbed two Jersey heifers around the necks and called them "dood fellows."

"Look out, boy, they might kick you," Hiram warned.

"No they won't. They're dood," repeated Frank.

At that point, one of the heifers *did* kick him, and young Frank was both disappointed and displeased.

"He wanted me to take a club and learn them better," Hiram wrote his sister.

About three months later, Gilbreth Knox became sick on

a frigid night in December 1871. Hiram wouldn't let anyone else handle the horse, and although he had a bad cold himself he bundled up in a greatcoat Martha had woven for him and sat until dawn in the horse's stall.

The stallion was better the next day, but Hiram went to bed with pneumonia, and three days later he was dead at the age of thirty-eight.

Martha felt that her life had ended, too. But she ultimately enjoyed her almost fifty years of widowhood. Only when she was a wrinkled, balding woman in her eighties did she begin to slow down at all.

"One thing I've promised myself," she wrote when she was in her eighties, after having visited a contemporary who she thought had surrendered to old age: "I won't hump nor scruff as long as I live. And when I die I'll lie straight in my casket."

No one ever heard Martha whine, either, at the time of her husband's death or later. Perhaps the closest she ever came to self-pity was when as an old woman she wrote on the last page of her reminiscences:

"My heart is still warm for the old town [North Anson] where I received my first impressions at the age of no responsibilities, when to me everybody and everything was good, and not even man was vile.

"I sometimes go back to visit it, but only the landscape is familiar—not one friend of my youth is there; entire families have passed on.

"I refresh my memory by visiting the graveyard, and as I read their names, some reminder of them comes to mind, and their faces I recall as in life. And when I leave them I feel almost as if I had seen them and talked with them."

Right after Hiram's death, Martha became seriously sick. Doctors attributed it to shock, and it took her almost a year to snap out of a lassitude that she herself was aware of, but couldn't explain. During that time, her Gilbreth in-laws helped her liquidate Hiram's estate. Gilbreth Knox alone fetched $18,000, and four of the stallion's colts fetched another $16,000—a small fortune by Maine standards. Those sums, when added to proceeds from the sale of the other animals and the general store, were deemed sufficient to support Martha and her three children comfortably.

I don't know what happened, exactly, after that, because neither my grandmother nor father would ever discuss it. But somehow or other one of Hiram's sisters or brothers-in-law either invested the funds and lost them, or actually misappropriated them. At any rate, after Martha recovered from her illness, she found that her fortune had dwindled to a few thousand dollars.

The matter never went to court, or anything like that. But Martha severed all ties with the Gilbreths; and Frank subsequently ignored them; and, when it gets down to my generation, I've never met one of them and don't even know if there *are* any of them.

The Bunkers, of course, quickly rallied around to help Martha. But she wouldn't take charity, even from relatives. Instead, she decided to pick up and move clear out of the State of Maine.

She selected Andover, Massachusetts, as an ideal town in which to raise children, because Phillips Andover for boys and Abbott Academy for girls were situated there. So she, her youngest sister Kit, and the three children moved to Andover, rented a house and moved in.

But by the time Frank was old enough to enter Phillips Andover, Hiram's estate had all but disappeared. Consequently Frank had to go to public schools after all.

They stayed in Andover for a few more years, and then Martha decided that they'd move to Boston, where the public schools were better than Andover's. By that time, she had attempted to instill a sense of responsibility in ten-year-old Frank, who still occasionally failed to measure up as the "man of the family."

On the morning that Martha, Kit, and the children were scheduled to move to Boston, Martha told her son:

"We're going to leave in two hours, on the eleven o'clock train, and I want you to be ready."

"All right, Marthie," he replied—and it was a name that no one else in the family dared use.

"I'm not joking, boy."

"All right, Pat," he promised—and that was another name no one else dared use.

"And if you're not here, we're going without you. Mind what I say."

Frank went out to say good-bye to his friends, and forgot to keep track of the time. When it dawned on him that more than two hours had passed, he returned sheepishly home to make his apologies—only to find the house locked and empty. So he hurried to the station, convinced that they wouldn't abandon him without a cent in his pocket.

The platform was empty, though, and an unsympathetic stationmaster confirmed that the family had gone to Boston without him.

"Didn't they even leave me a ticket?" Frank asked, on the verge of tears.

"Can't say they did, boy."

"Didn't they even seem to be *looking* for me?"

"I suspect they thought that any boy who wasn't on hand to help his widowed mother move wasn't hardly *worth* looking for."

"I," choked Frank, and you could tell this was the crowning blow, "haven't even had my lunch!"

"Do tell."

"And even if I should *get* to Boston, I don't know where the house is."

"Well, now there you're in luck. Your mother just happened to leave the address with me, in case I had to forward any baggage. And if you sweep out the waiting-room real good and then the baggage-room and then both platforms, I *might* find you some lunch and lend you the price of a ticket."

Somewhat subdued, Frank joined his family that night in Boston, where his mother made a great pretense of never having noticed he was gone.

"If it hadn't been for Mr. Phelps at the station," Frank finally blurted out, feeling very sorry for himself, "I'd still be in Andover—and without a thing to eat."

"Oh, he gave you something to eat?"

"He had some sandwiches—just like the kind you make."

"And he loaned you money for a ticket?"

Frank nodded.

"It's nice to have friends like Mr. Phelps," said Martha. "I've got some chores for you to do, so you can earn the money to pay him back."

"I hope it ain't sweeping," said Frank, holding up his palms and displaying some blisters.

Once when Dad told us that story in the presence of Grandma, someone asked:

"And weren't you scared, Daddy—all alone on the Andover rail platform?"

"Who, *me?* I should say not. I figured I was like one of those boys Horatio Alger writes about. I was going to enter the city without any money, hungry, and friendless. But I knew I'd make my pile."

"Humph!" Grandma allowed. "Blistered hands, and you

should have had a blistered bottom. My soul and body!"

"I'll bet that what Grandma was trying to do was to teach you never to be late to anything," one of us said.

"If that's what I was trying, I was a mighty poor teacher," Martha muttered. "Man and boy, I'd say he's been late for meals at least twenty thousand times since the day we left Andover. And one of these days, when he doesn't come when he's called, he's not going to *get* any dinner."

We knew that Dad's being late to the table was a source of annoyance to both her and my mother. But he always explained his tardiness by saying he couldn't stand for his food to be too hot.

"After that, Daddy," we persisted, "were you ever late for a train again?"

"Well, I'll admit that occasionally—maybe every ten years or so—I may be a few seconds late for something," he conceded. "But being on time wasn't the lesson I learned from your Grandma in Andover. No, siree Bob! What I learned was that when you don't know whether or not she's bluffing, you'd better not call her hand. Eh, Pat?"

"I should have skinned you alive," scowled Grandma, whose threats of dire discipline often revolved about human taxidermy and blistered or tanned backsides, with occasional red-Indian scalpings executed so expertly that the victims were invariably left balder than the state house dome. Although actually she had mellowed into a gentle, lovable creature, she still enjoyed picturing herself now and then as a ruthless remover or heater of quivering epidermis.

When Grandma thought one of us required discipline, she'd order us to march right out into the yard and cut her a switch from the lilac bush. Naturally, we'd cut the smallest twig we thought we could get away with. She'd swing this viciously through the air, purposely missing us by inches, while informing us that our bottoms would soon be in such painful shape we'd have to eat off the mantlepiece. Sometimes she'd land a light blow or two, and we'd dutifully flinch, holler murder, and cringe away from her like beaten curs, so that she wouldn't lose face.

"I'll teach you to mind your manners," she'd threaten darkly, as the twig whistled harmlessly past that part of the anatomy she had vowed to furrow. "I've a mind to take the hide right off you. *There!* How do you like *that!* And *that!* And *that!*"

"Mercy! Have mercy!" we'd yelp.

As a middle-aged woman in Boston, though, Martha had mellowed very little. Still tactless and outspoken, she had the straight-backed, forbidding bearing of a New England matriarch.

The only thing she was trained for was teaching school. But the pay scale for teachers in Boston was slightly less than $500 a year, and she knew she couldn't support her three children and Kit on that. So she decided to open a boardinghouse.

First, though, with the eyes of a former schoolteacher, she surveyed Boston to determine which district had the best schools. And when she had made up her mind on that, she started to look at vacant houses in the district.

At last she located an empty, five-story, pre-Civil War residence on Columbus Avenue, which seemed ideal. But the rent was a thousand dollars a year, payable in advance, and Martha and Kit between them couldn't raise a hundred.

So Martha put on her best clothes, went to a Boston bank, and somehow—with no security or co-signers—came out with a check for the thousand. The only guarantee she could offer was her stern and rockbound face and her straight spine. But they were enough.

"The bank president asked me how I knew I could run a boardinghouse," Martha once said, "and I told him that *any* woman raised in the State of Maine could run one."

Few people enjoyed eating more than Martha, so the dining room of her boardinghouse was unsurpassed. Also, she believed that cleanliness was next to godliness, and that drinking and adultery were the devil's strongest magnets. So within a matter of months, every room in the house was filled—and the project was a complete success.

The days of the splendid, ultra-respectable boardinghouse are gone, but for many years the institution was a vital part of the American scene. And the immaculate boardinghouse of Victorian days should not be confused with its fleabag survivor of present times.

The old-time boardinghouse was a residence, a restaurant, a club, a protector of morals, and a place where a respectable stranger could become acquainted. Martha was the ideal proprietress: moral, clean, fair, interested but not a nosy Parker, friendly but not over-familiar.

Usually she could size up persons who applied for rooms, and tell whether they would make congenial tenants. When in doubt, she asked for references. On those rare occasions when she made a mistake and admitted someone who strayed from the straight-and-narrow, she did not follow that maxim about every dog—especially a gay one—being entitled to one bite. The offender would hear a firm knock on his door, and when he opened it, there would be the forbidding figure of Martha Gilbreth, chin extended, shoulders braced, back stiff, and lips pursed.

The offender invariably grasped the reason for her visit,

even before she pointed downstairs in the general direction of the front door and intoned, "Out!"

Usually the offender departed quickly and quietly—and presumably the better off morally for having experienced Martha's withering and well-merited contempt.

"One toot and you're 'oot,' " her Irish domestics used to titter to each other—the "oot" apparently being their version of how a Maine native pronounced "out."

A whole parade of these girls was brought over from Ireland, to do the housework and cooking. Besides seeing to it that they gave her the New England version of an honest day's work, Martha made sure they bathed, kept their clothes clean, and wrote their parents at least once a month. When they drew their pay, she supervised how they spent it, and went with them to buy their clothes. She also made sure, when they went out courting on an evening off, that their beaux were single and had jobs. If the girls were brought home late, Martha told the beaux not to come back.

Aunt Kit was so engrossed in her painting that she was no help at running the boardinghouse. She was quite a talented artist, but not good enough to make a living from her canvases, which were in demand for displays but rarely sold.

Martha didn't really want or need any help, though, and she was even more proud of Kit's work than Kit herself. So Martha kept encouraging her younger sister to keep painting.

As for Martha's three children, Anne became so skilled at the piano that she won a scholarship and went abroad to study with Franz Liszt. Mary, who spent hours in the public library reading books on botany, led her class at the Latin High School for Girls. Frank, unfortunately, was far from a brilliant student—particularly in spelling.

"As a former teacher, you've heard the expression about a

child who couldn't spell 'cat,' " one of Frank's discouraged teachers complained to Martha. "Well here, for the first time in my experience, is a boy who literally can't."

Frank was extremely dexterous, though. With a few strokes of a pencil, he could draw figures which seemed to be in motion. He could write upside down and backwards, simultaneously, with both hands. From an old broomstick, he could carve an intricate wooden chain, or a series of balls rolling in a framework as long as the broomstick itself.

"Sometimes, boy, I think you were born twenty years too late," Martha used to tell him. "On a whaling ship, you'd be the world's champion scrimshaw man. But in a Boston school, you're at the foot of the class."

I remember once, when my father was chiding me for a bad report card, Grandma dug into what she called her "hopeless chest" and produced a copy of a spelling test he had taken as a boy. Out of twenty-six words, he had missed a magnificent total of twenty-four.

"What did your teacher say, when she saw how stupid you were?" I couldn't resist asking him.

"*Stupid!*" he protested smugly. "Lord love a duck. Who said anything about being stupid? I simply told her that, within a couple of years after I graduated from high school, I'd hire a battery of secretaries to do my spelling for me."

"Go along!" Grandma corrected him. "You couldn't have found anybody in those days, including yourself, who thought you were even going to get *into* high school, let alone graduate from it."

Besides spelling, Frank was also poor in grammar and awful in French, although he excelled in mathematics and mechanical drawing. He attended the Rice Training School, an experimental institution where new ideas and teaching methods were tried—and was taught the metric system before he became familiar with feet, pounds and so forth. Possibly because of this, he subsequently urged adoption of the metric system in the United States.

He finally learned how to spell—and in fact became an excellent speller. But he still thought that schools had to waste a lot of valuable time teaching the subject, and so he also became actively connected with organizations advocating simplified spelling. In fact he tried to use simplified spelling in the books he wrote, but his publishers wouldn't agree.

He also was active in sponsoring the universal language, Esperanto. Incidentally, he gave up altogether trying to learn French, but he spent his whole life trying to master German. Lillie, of course, spoke it fluently. There was a time when he hired both a German governess for the children and a German tutor for himself—and also asked Lillie to speak German around the house. But very little of it rubbed off on him.

Once during a management meeting in Berlin, he tried to read his speech in German—and someone interrupted him politely to inquire what language he was speaking. And there was one horribly embarrassing occasion at a German banquet, where he had carefully prepared a toast in German, but inadvertently used an unprintable word when he meant to say "delicious repast."

Frank got such poor grades in the Rice School that Martha, in exasperation, finally kept him home and tutored him. She was such a good teacher that he was soon making excellent progress.

"He can do long division in half the time—no, a *quarter* of the time—of any other child that I have ever taught," Martha wrote one of her brothers.

By the time Frank entered the new English High School, he was well prepared in all subjects except French, which he dropped. By his junior year, he had even mastered spelling, and was at the top of his class in math and science. Also, he designed and built a sporty, double-runner sled, which was the talk of the school and which won a prize at an exhibit of the Mechanics Institute.

A flip letter which he wrote his mother at that time doesn't contain a single spelling error. He had been visiting at a farm outside of Boston, and he told Marthie:

"In the parlor there is an organ, and on the wall a marriage certificate and their pictures. . . . Everything is so neat you can see your face in it—even the back of Mr. S's coat. . . . I went to the barn and studied animal nature until I caught on how to get cow juice. The first time I got the thing a-working, it slipped around and squirted me in the eye. . . ."

During the spring of his senior year, when he was sixteen, he passed entrance examinations to the Massachusetts Institute of Technology.

"I outsmarted them on a question," he told us on one occasion. "The exam paper read, 'Can you conjugate the French verb meaning "to go"?' and I answered, 'I can.' So they couldn't do anything but mark it correct."

"Well, if you *could* conjugate it, why didn't you just conjugate it?" I asked—and I wasn't trying to needle him, merely trying to find out. "It would have been a better thing to do."

"But the point was," he explained patiently, "that I couldn't really conjugate it, but I didn't want to get marked wrong. So you see, I outsmarted them by . . ."

"By *what?*" Grandma interrupted him. "Exactly what I told your father! By telling a big fat lie, that's what."

"When some people tell a lie," Dad mumbled, "it's a 'story' or at worst a 'fib.' But on those extremely rare occasions when I stretch the truth a little, it's always big and fat. Maybe the only person I outsmarted was myself—when I decided to tell the story to you kids."

Shortly before he graduated from high school, Frank had some second thoughts about going to college. Principally, he wanted to relieve Martha of the chore of running a boardinghouse—although the fact was that she rather enjoyed the challenge of this. I don't think it ever entered her mind that the running of such an establishment might be a step down the social scale. Regardless of whatever opinion the dowagers of Boston may have had, Martha always felt that Maine natives—especially those descended from Governors Bradford and Dudley—were as good as anybody "and a sight better than most."

Meanwhile, Frank was being urged by a Boston building contractor to pass up M.I.T. and come to work for him. The contractor, Renton Whidden, was Frank's Sunday School teacher at the Unitarian Church. Whidden had been impressed by the sled Frank had built, and also by his general mechanical ability and the way he managed to get along with people.

Mr. Whidden was looking for a young native American to serve as foreman of a crew of Irish immigrants. Foremen rarely came from the ranks of the immigrants themselves, because most employers looked on "foreigners" as "agitators" who couldn't be trusted in jobs of responsibility.

Mr. Whidden promised to waive apprenticeship restrictions, and to move Frank right up the ladder, if he'd sign on as a laborer and learn the various construction trades. And if Frank measured up, there might even be an offer of a partnership.

Bricklayers were making three dollars a day, which was good pay in 1885, and Frank *did* want to get his family out of the boardinghouse. So he bought a pair of white overalls and a blue denim shirt, and announced to his disappointed mother and horrified aunt and sisters that he had "accepted a position" as a bricklayer's helper.

"First a boardinghouse," complained Aunt Kit, "and now a bricklayer's helper in the family. What next?"

Since she didn't contribute to the family's support, she didn't have much right to complain. But Martha had made it plain to her children that they were to treat Aunt Kit with respect. So nobody gave her a short answer.

Martha had learned that, as Frank grew older, his decisions were usually right and that, at any rate, there wasn't much use arguing once he had made up his mind. So all she said was:

"Well, then, if you're going to be a bricklayer's helper, for mercy's sake be a *good* bricklayer's helper."

"I'll do my best to try to find a good bricklayer to help," Frank teased her.

The next day, July 12, 1885, Frank rode to work on a horsecar, wearing his spotless overalls and carrying a dinner pail containing his mother's idea of what constituted a snack to assuage the midday hunger tantrums of a workingman —which is to say approximately enough to feed a Chinese family for a year.

Mr. Whidden assigned him to help his fastest and best bricklayer, a wiry Irishman named Tom Bowler, who liked to quote Shakespeare and could chin himself with either hand. Tom wasn't at all sure he liked the idea of being helped by the boss's protégé. And a couple of times, when Frank got in his way, the Irishman "accidentally" spattered the new overalls with mortar.

Frank figured that he'd be lucky if that was the only initiation he received. Meanwhile, anxious to learn, he was studying methods. And for the first time he became interested in what was to be his life work: Motion Study.

Frank noticed that the bricklayer used three entirely different sets of motions: one when he was laying slowly but steadily; a second when he put on a burst of speed to impress someone; and a third when he was working very slowly and trying to teach his helper.

When Frank pointed this out, Tom thought he was criticizing his ability as a teacher, and spattered the boy's shoes as well as his overalls.

"I don't see why a smart kid like you wants to lay bricks in the first place," said Tom, with a sarcasm that was lost on Frank.

"Well, you see," Frank replied in a rush of enthusiasm, "I'm studying to be a contractor myself."

"Say, now ain't that *nice*," said Tom. "Seventeen years old, you said you was. And your mother runs a boardinghouse. And you ain't even trained to be a bricklayer's helper yet. And on your first day at work you're talking about going into business for yourself."

"That's right," grinned Frank, who either missed or chose to ignore the sarcasm.

"And will you give me a job, lad?"

"You bet your sweet life," the boy told him magnanimously. "Anybody who could lay brick like you could get a job anywhere he wanted."

Ten years later, when Frank *did* go into business for himself, Tom Bowler became his right-hand man, and the two were associated for years. But despite Frank's compliment, they didn't hit it off too well on that first day.

"Why don't you show me the same way you do it yourself," Frank kept asking.

Tom thought that was exactly what he *was* doing. "Dammit, boy, just do what I tell you, and keep your mouth shut," he ordered.

"But do you know you're laying brick three different ways?"

" 'The fool doth think he is wise, but the wise man knows himself to be a fool,' " Tom quoted the bard. "If you open your mouth again about my bricklaying, I'll lay a brick in it."

"But you *are* using different ways."

"You're the one who came here to learn," Tom hollered. "For Christ's sake, boy, don't try to learn us!"

"I'm sorry, honest," Frank apologized. "But don't you see that if one of your ways is right, then the other two have *got* to be wrong."

"I told you onest!" Tom threatened. " 'Cudgel thy brains no more.' " He tossed a blob of mortar that plopped dead-center into Frank's mouth!

A few days later, Frank was assigned to another ace brick-layer, George Eaton, a Nova Scotian, who also was to become an important part of the Gilbreth contracting business. Frank noticed that George also had three different sets of motions—and that all were different from Tom's.

Analyzing his initial week at work, Frank wrote in the first of a series of memo books that he always carried with him, "I decided to use the right motions, even if the brick was laid crooked. Then if the brick *was* crooked, I'd stop and straighten it. But I wasn't going to get into the habit of using wrong motions."

And there, on paper, were Frank's first precepts of Motion Study.

Because he had to stop to straighten crooked bricks, Frank was the slowest apprentice on the job for the first few months. In fact his foreman used to tell him he was probably the slowest in Massachusetts. But Frank finally developed a smooth set of motions, incorporating the best of Tom's and George's techniques, and then there weren't any crooked bricks to straighten.

He also discovered that he could lay bricks much faster—and with much less effort—by having the unlaid bricks and the mortar on a level with the work area. And since there was no scaffold which provided this, he designed a makeshift one. In so doing, he cut the motions required to lay one brick from eighteen to five.

Tom and George were both alert enough to appreciate what he was doing, and began to work with him. They helped him smooth out his motions, and suggested improvements to the scaffold. They still liked to needle him, though.

"Dammit, lad, you ain't smart," Tom used to say. "You're just too Goddamned lazy to squat, that's all."

"A man had ought to be ashamed to draw his pay, making things that easy for himself," George added. "Why don't you bring a pillow to set on."

A year later, at the age of eighteen, Frank was the fastest bricklayer on the job. A journeyman was supposed to lay a hundred and seventy-five an hour. Frank could *coast* and lay three hundred and fifty. Workers from other projects would sometimes come over to watch the kid perform. Occasionally, Frank would showboat-it-up for the visitors, flipping his trowel pancake fashion, and making the mortar fly, while his hod-carrier was hard pressed to keep him supplied with bricks.

Sometimes, too, a contest would be arranged after hours between Frank and a speed-merchant on another job. Tom, George, and Frank would pool their funds, and bet the works on "the kid." Frank never failed to win—mostly because of the scaffold—and the three would celebrate by buying a keg of beer and inviting everyone on the job to join them.

Mr. Whidden was impressed not only by Frank's speed but by the way he got along with the other men. The contractor transferred Frank from trade to trade. He learned to be a carpenter, a plumber, a furnace-installer, a glazier. All-in-all, he drew journeyman's pay at more than fifty trades. Just before he was twenty he was made an assistant foreman, and he did so well in that capacity that within a few months he was promoted to foreman. At twenty-one—when he would have been graduating if he had gone to M.I.T.—he was named a full-fledged superintendent. So his overall days were finished, and he became a coat-stiff-collar-and-tie man.

Frank had a seemingly limitless supply of energy, and a driving desire to make enough money to move his family out of the boardinghouse. And that combination made him invaluable to Mr. Whidden, who had the jobs that needed desperately to be done—and was willing to pay for them.

Once, when bad weather put two Whidden jobs behind schedule, Frank superintended both of them at once. He'd stay on one job most of the day, and when it got dark he'd jump in a buggy and race to a nearby town, where he'd run the show until almost dawn.

Meanwhile, he perfected his bricklayer's scaffold, patented it, and offered it to other contractors for $100 a year. The scaffold caught on right away, and checks started to arrive in the mail.

"Enables the bricklayer to lay bricks *fastest*," said a pamphlet he circulated through the trade. "No time is lost in stooping . . . . And the contractor gets the benefit of it."

So as the money began to come in, Frank insisted that

Martha close the boardinghouse—although at first she was somewhat reluctant to do so.

"What happens when the scaffold money stops coming in?" she asked.

"Why then, Marthie," he beamed, "I'll invent something *else.*"

"I don't like to see you work so hard," she protested.

"Look, Marthie, *anybody* can make money who knows how to work. And *almost* anybody can make barrels of money if he knows how to make people work for him. You'll see."

So Martha closed the boardinghouse, and they moved to Brookline, a Boston suburb. Frank bought identical brass beds and identical mahogany rocking chairs for Martha and Kit, whom he called his duplicate mother. And for himself, he bought an overstuffed easy chair with a reclining back that he had long coveted. Now, when he was doing two jobs at once for Mr. Whidden, he could stretch out in the chair for a couple of hours' sleep, without going to bed.

The four women in his family had always spoiled him. When he became the main source of support—and they saw how hard he was working for all of them—they waited on him hand and foot.

Meanwhile, his two sisters were busy with careers of their own. Shortly after they moved to Brookline, Anne married and opened a music school in Providence. Mary Elizabeth was doing advanced work in botany, and corresponded regularly with Louis Agassiz, who was quick to recognize her talent. She was elected to the American Association for the Advancement of Science, and published a pamphlet entitled *Dissemination of Plants Chiefly by Their Seed,* with the blessing of Radcliffe College.

Just as Mary Elizabeth seemed ready to make an impact in her field, she was found to have an advanced case of tuberculosis, and died within three months. Her collection was presented to Radcliffe, where it was maintained intact for many years.

And so, now, Frank and his duplicate mothers lived alone in the Brookline house, where the two women vied with each other in pampering him, and where he enjoyed showering them with identical presents. Kit still had her painting to keep her busy. But Martha found time on her hands, now that the boardinghouse was closed. She was a great cook, and she occupied herself in fixing the special dishes that Frank liked best.

As Frank moved up the Whidden ladder and as the scaffold royalties accumulated, he was rapidly becoming an extremely eligible bachelor. And no one was more aware of that fact than his duplicate mothers—who watched developments very closely indeed, and with what must have been mixed emotions.

CHAPTER 6

Boston Bachelor

Mr. Whidden promoted Frank to chief superintendent, which was just one step below partner. And now, for the first time, word started to go through the building industry that young Gilbreth, the red-headed workhorse who could lay bricks so fast, had a way of getting extra work out of other people, too.

"That kid makes it 'aisy' for a man to work hard," one Irish laborer observed somewhat ruefully, after the quitting whistle blew.

The description was apt, and caught on quickly. Thereafter, not only the laborers but the other contractors would refer to him as the fellow who "makes it 'aisy' to work hard."

The "aisy" part of it was his insistence that all workers eliminate fatiguing and time-wasting motions. No one knew better than Frank what it was to be bone-tired. And although he wasn't at that time the sort of crusader that he became later, he still didn't think it was right to send men—especially old-timers—home so weary they could barely shuffle.

Analyzing each trade as he had bricklaying, Frank tried to eliminate or shorten motions by bringing building materials up to the working level, so that a man wouldn't have to squat, lift, or reach.

The result was that there was no longer any slowing up in the afternoons from exhaustion, and Frank's men would walk home with springs still left in their steps, after having done more work than they had ever done before.

Needless to say, the unions were observing all of this quite carefully, because jobs were scarce, and if a man became more productive he might deprive someone else of work. But Frank foresaw the huge industrial expansion of the country, and said that better pay and shorter hours would create the new jobs.

Frank himself belonged to a union and believed in unions. He had no use for men who refused to stand up and fight for their rights. He was convinced, too, that people who were adequately paid produced better than people who weren't. He also knew from personal experience that a man's pay could be stopped when bad weather closed a building project; and that construction workers often had no jobs at all in the winter, and felt elated when spring finally arrived and they could look forward to "two summers, with only one winter in between."

No one enjoyed the Gay Nineties more than Frank. He loved to eat, drink, ride horses and bicycles, squire pretty girls, go to the theater, and dance. His memo books and desk-reminder calendars of those days are almost embarrassingly laden with such cryptic notes as:

"Flowers for Esther"; "Candy for Flo"; "What about Esther?"; "Can Flo ride tandem?"; "Theater with B"; "Ask Susan"; "Does J like to dance?"

Those were the days when practically everyone in Boston rode bicycles—both to get places and simply for the fun of it. Girls and women in white middy-blouses and blue-serge bloomers, boys and men with garters on their shirtsleeves and clips on their pant-legs, went tooling or meandering along on their wheels, with handlebar bells tinkling gaily.

Ball-bearing bikes had only recently been introduced, and the original "bone-shakers" had been replaced by the smooth, easy-does-it "safeties." With a "safety" bicycle, you could coast, instead of having to pedal madly all the time.

Congressmen, governors, diplomats, educators, and scientists all over the country—along with the man-in-the-street —were spending delightful Sunday afternoons on their bicycles. The bicycle-picnic was a national institution, and except in the industrial cities the air was clear and wine-like.

Frank bought every new "safety" model as it appeared, and owned a tandem for his dates. He was among the first to complete the much-discussed "Century Run"—covering a hundred miles in fourteen hours. And an entry in one of his memo books notes that, on a jaunt with a male companion, "Ernest had to be carried home in a buggy, but I rode my machine back and must have covered seventy-five miles."

He also occasionally went by train to Brooklyn, New York, where he rode a tandem bike to Coney Island with his first cousin, Jane Bunker, who was studying to become a dentist. Jane was diminutive and vivacious—and both Martha and Kit began to downgrade her in their conversations with Frank, for fear he might be falling for her.

"No cousin!" Martha told him firmly, making it plain that Jane was out-of-bounds as a marriage partner.

For a time, Frank also squired a short but intelligent girl from one of Boston's best families, and Martha and Kit downgraded her by referring to her as "the dwarf." Then he became quite serious about a good-looking actress, and Martha and Kit decided that she might be Jewish, and from then on called her "the Jewess."

Apparently he also squired a widow, because I remember that he and Grandma used to joke about a one-time ukase of hers that went, "No cousin, no dwarf, no Jewess, no widow."

He always put his work before his social life, however, and often he'd labor at home, far into the night, on some idea of his own, after having put in a twelve- or fourteen-hour-day for Mr. Whidden.

One result of his homework was the Gilbreth Waterproof Cellar, which he patented in the winter of 1895, and which prevented leaks in concrete substructures. He issued a calendar which listed high tides for the year, and also advertised his cellar.

"High tides make cellars wet; we make them dry," the calendar announced.

This worked out so well that he decided to leave the Whidden organization and go into the contracting business for himself. So on April 1, 1895, he opened an office at 85 Water Street, in downtown Boston—and went to it faithfully every morning. But for four long months, he failed to land a single contract.

During those months, he'd sometimes joke grimly with Martha and Kit about the "jackass who went into business for himself on April Fool's Day." But neither he nor Martha ever had any real doubt about his making good on his own. And Aunt Kit kept her thoughts to herself.

When he finally landed his first contract—to build a large waterproof cellar—he went home jubilantly and announced the news. Then he wired his sister Anne in Providence, "Landed first job. To 'ell with poverty."

After that, the jobs began to roll in. He got the contract for Prescott Hall in Cambridge. Next came the Webster Building on Warren Street. Then came a score of others, including the ten-story Women's Club House at 13 Beacon Street.

While still in his twenties, Frank became one of the largest contractors in the United States. On top of that, he made a small fortune on the Gilbreth Gravity Mixer, which he patented in 1899. This was a new type of concrete mixer, which vibrated as the materials descended by gravity.

When the manufacturer of an existing mixer challenged Frank's assertion that his machine was the best in the world, Frank ran newspaper advertisements demanding a public contest.

The competitor wrote Frank somewhat haughtily:

"Should we win, it would not raise the standard of our mixer. Hence we regret the necessity of declining to contest with you."

Then Frank bought newspaper ads to reproduce that quotation, and to assert that his competitor had in effect thrown in the sponge.

"Simply a matter of advertising and agents," Frank noted in his memo book, as he opened offices in London and a dozen other cities, to sell the mixer.

His contracting business grew rapidly, also, and he soon was building structures all the way from San Francisco to Berlin. He crossed the United States several times a year, and constructed the first tall buildings in close to a score of Western towns that were to become important cities.

And although he hadn't been able to attend M.I.T., he now had the satisfaction of being the subject of a convocation address at the college. M.I.T.'s president, Henry Smith Pritchett, used Frank's amazing speed record on the Lowell Laboratory as the theme of his convocation speech in 1902 and described Gilbreth as an "unusual and master builder." The *Boston Evening Transcript,* echoing these sentiments, said the eleven-week completion of the laboratory was a "marvel" of industrial planning and of cooperation between labor and management.

Frank was a month short of thirty-five and Lillie had just turned twenty-five, when they met in June 1903 at the Boston City Library.

Frank's California cousin, Minnie Bunker, did the honors.

Minnie was a daughter of Martha's oldest brother, Sam. She had moved from Maine to the West Coast as a girl, and now taught in the Oakland public schools. Enterprising and intelligent like all the offspring of the Tribe of Dan, Minnie liked to travel, and sometimes financed European trips by chaperoning young ladies on the Grand Tour.

Minnie died a few years ago, and was articulate and vigorous to the very end. Her age at the time of her death was a carefully guarded secret. So, although I came across her birthdate and the year she graduated from Colby College in research for this book, I shall not give her away here.

My best recollection of Cousin Minnie involves an embarrassing incident during the last days of World War II. I telephoned her when I was passing through San Francisco en route home from the Pacific, and she insisted on seeing me. She was going to preside at some banquet in a San Francisco hotel that night, and I was to send a waiter to summon her.

I did as I was bid. I was wearing a Navy uniform, and it

so happened that standing near me was a crusty-looking rear admiral, about twice my age and also in uniform.

Minnie, whose eyes weren't quite what they used to be and who knew nothing about uniforms or rank insignia, barged up to the admiral, threw her arms about him, kissed him full on the lips, and proclaimed:

"You dear, *dear* boy, you don't know what this means to me. I would have known you *anywhere*. You're the image of your dear father, when he was your age. And who could miss those Bunker eyes?"

"What the hell," quavered the admiral, trying Laocoön fashion to disengage himself, "goes on here?" He backed up a couple of steps, but Minnie was reluctant to turn him loose.

"You dear, *dear* boy," she repeated.

I think the admiral had a dreadful suspicion that he was being compromised by some superannuated Mata Hari, or that he was the pigeon of a pickpocket scheme. At any rate, the color went out of his cheeks, and he sputtered rather loudly that he had never seen the "old bat" before in his life.

Minnie was old, all right, but anything but a bat. In fact, she was a gracious lady, and I suppose I should have taken the admiral to task. But by then I had already learned enough about admirals to know that if he should find out I was in any way associated with Minnie, I might well spend the next twenty years regretting it. And I had no desire at that point to have my leave canceled or to spend those twenty years with a broomstick tipped by a nail, picking up the debris around the officer's mess at some outpost like Guam.

So I faded away, and made believe I hadn't seen the incident. A few minutes later, after the admiral had departed, I caught Minnie in another part of the lobby—and tapped her on the shoulder.

"Cousin Minnie?" I asked.

She threw her arms around me, and went through the act and speech all over again, as if nothing had happened.

Minnie had my mother and three other girls in tow when she arrived in Boston en route to Europe in 1903. Their ship was to sail from Boston, and they had a couple of days to kill. Part of Minnie's job was to keep the girls amused, so she asked her Cousin Frank to take two of them—Eva Powell and Lillie—for a sight-seeing tour in his new Winton Six.

Eva and Lillie were on the second floor of the Boston Library, studying the Abbey murals of Sir Launfal and the Holy Grail, when Minnie walked up with Frank.

"Ladies," said Minnie, "may I present my cousin, Mr. Frank Gilbreth."

And that was that. If any bells rang or electric shocks ran up anyone's spine, neither Lillie nor Frank ever recorded that phenomenon.

Minnie's brother Fred, who still lived in Maine, had come to Boston to see her, so he was drafted as the second escort.

"But I had your father picked to escort your mother," Minnie once told us when we were children. "Fred was the escort for Eva."

"And did you think right then that they would someday get married?" we asked.

"Gracious peace! I should say not. Your father was what was known, back in those days, as 'not the marrying kind.' After all, he was thirty-five. And between him and his mother—not to mention your Great Aunt Kit—he had managed to elude most of the girls in Boston. And as for your mother, she was so shy no one thought she was even *interested* in catching a man."

"Then why did you pick Dad to escort Mother?"

"Because I thought everyone—your father, your mother, and *especially* your Cousin Minnie," said Cousin Minnie, "would find it interesting to see what happened when the irresistible force met the immovable body. So . . ."

Minnie and the four young people went for a ride around Boston in the Winton that June night. Minnie wanted Frank to drive them through the Harvard campus and show them the sites of historic interest. But for the most part Frank pointed out building projects: his own and those of other contractors. There were Gilbreth signs on six different jobs, and as they chugged by Frank would say:

"That one will be ready in another ten days, if the weather stays good." And, "I was awfully lucky to get this job. Twenty-five other people bid on it."

He wasn't bragging in the least. He simply believed that everyone—even two pampered young ladies from California —would be just as interested in stressed concrete and steel beams as he was. And because he talked well and had a contagious enthusiasm, Lillie was fascinated.

In a brief biography of Frank, entitled *The Quest of the One Best Way,* written a few months after his death, Lillie made only one reserved reference to this first meeting.

"It was interesting to a girl," she wrote, "to see the town and its environments through his eyes; to learn of strength of materials and the problem of construction. . . ."

The next day, Frank invited the group to have tea with Martha, Kit, and himself, at their house on Boylston Street. Lillie wrote in *The Quest:* "It was a charming house—that of the young man and his 'duplicate mothers' whose chief joy and activities in life were making him happy. It was in this home that the girl he was to marry saw him among his own people—a family idol, waited on by inches, never asked to raise a finger, who found always a smiling welcome, a bountifully spread table, keen admiration."

Martha and Kit sat in their identical mahogany rockers and entertained the group cordially.

"You certainly have an attractive place, Mr. Gilbreth," Lillie said primly.

"I never knew a bachelor who had such good care taken of him," Minnie teased. "All he has to do is raise a finger, and *two* women wait on him."

"What else could anyone ask?" gloated Frank.

"Children," Lillie said quietly. Then, realizing how tactless the remark must have sounded, she started to blush. "I mean," she added lamely, "some people think that children are nice, too."

"Look at Miss Moller blush!" chortled Frank.

Martha didn't say anything. But Kit said with an intensity that surprised everyone, "If he wants children, his sister Anne has two he can play with. And they don't live so very far from Boston—only in Providence."

"Oh, I see," said Lillie, eager to get the conversation on another track. "Well, of course I didn't know about that. Yes, this certainly *is* an attractive place."

For some reason, although she had long since decided on a life of spinsterhood, Lillie had a premonition she was going to marry Frank Gilbreth. And the prospect of having two duplicate mothers-in-law from the State of Maine, who were sitting there straight-backed in their identical rockers, was frightening almost to the extent of terror.

CHAPTER 7

An Efficient Engagement

Terrified or not, Lillie was smitten. The next day was a perfect Sunday, and she and Eva went to church. After that, they were just sitting down for dinner at their hotel, the Parker House, when a bellboy brought in a card which said, "FBG and the buzz-wagon."

Eva wanted to eat first, but Lillie didn't think they ought to keep Frank waiting, so they canceled their orders and met him in the lobby. They picked up Minnie and Fred, and this time Frank had dusters and goggles for everyone, so they could go tooling across the countryside without getting dirty.

"Get a horse, twenty-three skiddoo!" the rural populace inevitably shouted, as the Winton left Boston in a cloud of dust, going like sixty.

These and other rude shouts ruffled Frank's none-too-smooth temper, but he was on his best behavior, and he managed to ignore them.

"Get that stinkpot off the highway!"

Frank still managed to keep quiet, although his lips were drawn tightly together.

"Say, Noah, what are you doing with that Ark?"

Frank stepped on the brakes, leaped from the car, and hollered at the retreating back of his taunter:

"Why, you damn fool, I'm collecting animals like the good Lord told me to. Now all I need is a jackass, so hop in, you Goddamned . . ."

"Why Mr. *Gil*-breth!" Lillie reproved him.

"Sorry," Frank grinned. "Well, now you girls have seen me the way I really am—at my worst. So I'm all through being on my best behavior."

After that, his relaxed manner and his quick laugh made Lillie forget her shyness. And pretty soon she was laughing as quickly and almost as loudly as he. Now, when anyone hollered, "Get a horse!", the whole group, including dignified Cousin Minnie, would shout back over their shoulders the time-worn rejoinder, "Pardon my dust!"

As Frank swerved from one side of the road to the other, to avoid hitting chickens whose protesting squawks could be heard above the rattle of the engine, Cousin Fred took over the chore of blowing the big bulb-horn. And Cousin Minnie retrieved a flying tailfeather, put it jauntily in her hat, got the giggles, and finally had hiccups.

But, as was its wont, the Winton inevitably coughed, coughed again, backfired, sighed, and then quit altogether. Frank and Fred got out and pushed it to the side of the road. Cars were still so uncommon in rural Massachusetts that a fairly large crowd of children soon gathered. While Frank and Fred probed experimentally among the various petcocks and valves under the hood, a number of urchins started to climb over the vehicle, thus making it rock. Meanwhile, on the adult fringes of the group, that old standby was making the rounds about autos not being here to stay.

The situation was ready-made for Lillie, who had that uncanny knack for managing children. She moved away from the car, propped her goggles up on her forehead, tucked her skirts and duster around her, and sat down in the shade of a maple tree. Then she beckoned to a couple of young children and, miraculously, they came and sat beside her. Quietly, and without any trace of theatrics, she started to tell them some stories from *Alice in Wonderland*. Before long, she was surrounded by twenty or twenty-five children, all listening intently.

With the children out of the way, Frank and Fred managed to get the Winton running again. But the children didn't want to let Lillie go until she had finished her story, so the two men sat, and listened to the windup.

Later, when they were tooling along the dusty countryside again, Frank asked the name of the story.

"Why it was *Alice in Wonderland!*" said Lillie.

"You mean kids really would listen to *that?*" Frank exclaimed. "Kids must be different than when I was a boy. Honestly, you had them hanging around like the Pied Piper. I never could get into *Alice in Wonderland,* myself."

"You really should read it," said Lillie. "It's a classic."

"If you say so, Miss Lillie, I'll read it. In fact you've impressed me so—getting those brats out of the way—that from now on I'll do everything you suggest."

"Now's your chance, Lillie," put in Cousin Minnie. "You'd better suggest something quickly, while you have all these witnesses. After all, we sail tomorrow."

"I suggest," said Lillie—and it was the most forward request she had ever made to a man—"that you drive us all to the boat tomorrow, in the buzz-wagon."

"Look at her blush," chortled Frank, for the second time. "I'll certainly do it, though."

He kept his word the next day, and drove them to the dock. But because of a supply problem at one of his building projects, he was so late that he found Minnie and the four girls standing nervously on the sidewalk in front of the Parker House—and they just barely made the boat.

"I'll meet your boat when you come back," he told Lillie as he hurried them toward the gangway.

"Is that a promise?" she asked almost coquettishly.

"Sure it is! Wild horses couldn't keep me away."

"I'll remember that."

"What do you mean?"

"We're not even coming to Boston. The boat lands in New York."

"All right," Frank said expansively. "I'll meet her in New York, then."

Frank shook hands impartially all around. And from what he had just said, you couldn't tell whether he planned to meet the boat because he was interested in anyone in particular, or simply because he enjoyed the collective company of Minnie and her California girls.

Lillie was bowled over, though, and Minnie was acute enough to recognize the symptoms. Minnie's job, after all, was to protect the young ladies—and surely that included preventing them from falling in love with thirty-five-year-old bachelor building contractors, with long strings of conquests.

So, for Lillie's benefit, Minnie dreamed up an entirely imaginary reason why Frank remained single.

"Yes, he's attractive," Minnie told her girls on the boat to Europe. "It's too bad that he'll never marry. You see, he was madly in love at one time with a perfectly beautiful girl—and she died a week before their wedding date. Consumption, I think. Anyway, he vowed at her bedside that he'd never marry anyone."

The story is so patently contrived that the wonder is Lillie could possibly take it seriously. Of course she had been sheltered all her life, and her principal knowledge of romance had come from Victorian novels.

At any rate, she *did* take it seriously—so seriously that she tried to put Frank altogether out of her thoughts. Only in Paris, where a postcard from him was waiting, did her hopes rise momentarily. But then she learned that the other three girls and Minnie had received cards, too.

Three months later, when their liner was being nuzzled by tugs into the dock at New York, Lillie stood at the rail and finally managed to distinguish her parents among the waving throng. Yes, there they were! She waved and threw them a kiss. And there were two of her sisters, Elinor and Ernestine. And Eva Powell's parents. And the derby-clad dandy in the midst of the group—who obviously had introduced himself and seemed very much at home—was Frank Gilbreth. So he hadn't forgotten, after all.

The whole group attended a dinner party that night, given by Lillie's parents, and then went to see the Broadway hit *Ben Hur.*

"I like your young man, Lillie-dear," Grosie told her daughter that night in their hotel.

"He's not *my* young man, Mama-dear," Lillie protested.

"He came all the way down from Boston to meet your boat, but he's not your young man!" Grosie protested. "Well, he's certainly *somebody's* young man."

"He likes us *all,*" Lillie maintained primly. "Remember, Miss Bunker is his first cousin. Anyway, he's never going to marry because he once was in love with a beautiful girl who died of consumption, you see, and he vowed . . ."

"On her deathbed," Grosie put in.

"How in the world did you know *that?*" Lillie asked incredulously.

"Lillie, *do!*" chortled Grosie. "Honestly! Did he tell you that?"

"No, but that's what Miss Bunker said. After all, they're first cousins, and . . ."

"My soul and body!" Grosie sighed. "Sometimes, Lillie-dear, I don't think you can see your hand in front of your face."

"I tell you, he likes us *all!*" Lillie protested.

But the next afternoon, Frank escorted her, all by herself, to the Metropolitan Museum of Art. And a couple of weeks later, he appeared at the hotel in Chicago where the Mollers were spending a few days, en route back to California.

"He meets your boat in New York, and then he follows you to Chicago, but he *still* isn't your young man," Grosie teased.

"He didn't exactly follow me," Lillie explained. "He's building a new factory here, so he had to come anyway. He's going to take me to see it this afternoon."

"That's nice, dear."

"And he asked me to go to the theater tonight. Do you think that's all right? I told him I'd have to ask you and Papa."

Grosie mulled it over. "He seems to be very nice," she conceded. "And after all, you *are* twenty-five. I guess if your father and I haven't taught you by now how to behave like a lady, you'll never learn. So go ahead, dear, and accept. I'll speak to Papa about it."

Lillie did a pirouette. "I'm glad you think he's nice,

Mama-dear," she said. "Do you think it's a coincidence he came to Chicago just when we did?"

"I don't *think* so," said Grosie, "but I could be wrong. I can tell you better when we get home."

"What do you mean, Mama-dear?"

"Well, if he suddenly shows up in Oakland, it's no coincidence."

A week before Christmas, the telephone rang in the Mollers' house, and Grosie answered it. Frank had just arrived from the East Coast, and obviously had done his homework on *Alice in Wonderland.* Mistaking Grosie's voice for Lillie's, he chirped:

"This is the White Rabbit from Boston."

Grosie identified herself. When Frank sheepishly asked to speak to Miss Lillie, Grosie requested his name.

"Mr. W. Rabbit of Boston," he said meekly.

For the next four days, Frank and Lillie inspected construction jobs, and went sight-seeing and to the theater— until Lillie thought there weren't any more sights to see.

"It was Christmas Eve, and your father still hadn't proposed," Mother used to tell us, "so I decided I'd better take *drastic action!* Christmas Eve and Christmas didn't seem the right time, because a lot was going on and I wanted his undivided attention. So I decided to wait until the day after Christmas and take him to the most romantic place I could think of—a park bench I had already picked out in San Francisco, overlooking the Golden Gate."

They took the ferry that day to San Francisco, and then a trolley. They spent the afternoon at an art gallery, and just as the sun started to set they passed the bench Lillie had in mind.

"Should we sit down and rest for just a minute?" she asked demurely. "I think I have something in my shoe."

They sat, she found an imaginary pebble in a shoe, and Frank did what was known as pop the question. When Lillie said yes, she received what I have every reason to believe was the first serious kiss of her life. Then he opened a Tiffany box, and put a ring on her finger.

"It's beautiful," she said. "But you were pretty sure of yourself, weren't you—bringing this all the way from New York."

"Not sure," Frank corrected her. "Just hopeful."

"Then there never was a solemn vow to another girl?"

"What are you talking about?"

"Did you ever court a girl who died of consumption?"

"Not that I know of. Why?"

"Never mind," Lillie sighed happily. "Merely asking, that's all."

Frank made it plain then that Martha and Kit would always have to live with them. Lillie dreaded that part of it, because she had a vivid memory of their Boston house, with the two New England women sitting straight in their identical rockers; with Kit's paintings on the walls and Martha's crocheted covers on the chairs; with everything arranged just as Frank liked it, and every meal composed of his favorite dishes, and served as if he were a royal nabob.

Lillie felt tremendously relieved, though, when Frank added that he intended to move from Boston to New York, where most of his new business was developing. So at least she wouldn't have to "move in" with the duplicate mothers, perhaps rooting one of them out of a bedroom. In effect, they'd be moving in with her. And that would be bad enough, but perhaps not utterly horrible. Anyway, for the time being she dismissed it from her mind.

They held hands all the way back to Oakland, where

Frank had a brief and formal talk with Papa. Then they broke the news to Grosie and the family, and finally to old Grandma Delger, who still was the hearty matriarch of the clan, and who still thought of Lillie as the mouselike little girl too shy to ask for her share of ladyfingers.

"Vell, now, so you got a man!" Grandma Delger enthused. "Dot's fine. I vant to giff you both der engagement party. Vot do you like to eat, young man?"

No one, not even Mrs. Delger, could be any more hearty than Frank when it came to talking about food. "What do I like to eat?" he repeated, tilting his head back for a loud guffaw. "Everything from a horse to the kitchen sink. Except onions."

"Dot's fine," Grandma Delger nodded enthusiastically. Then remembering that Lillie was a teetotaler and doubtless had selected a non-drinker as her fiancé, she asked a trifle skeptically:

"And vot do you like to drink?"

"Everything but glue," said Frank.

"Ah-ha!" gloated Mrs. Delger, looking at her granddaughter with new interest. "Dot's der fellow!"

It wasn't until Lillie was preparing for bed that night, and took off the ring for the first time, that she noticed the inscription—FBG and LEM, Dec. 26, 1903." So not only had he been sure of her, but he had the exact time all planned, too. And she had thought she was so clever, arranging the stop at the park bench and all.

For a few minutes she felt hurt. But, she finally told herself, he *did* pride himself on planning ahead and being efficient. And, after all, he *was* in the kind of business where you sometimes shipped in the materials before you signed the contract. But just the same . . .

"It didn't happen very often," Mother told us, "but that was one time when I really felt that your father—as Grosie once said about me—was just a little *too* efficient."

As for Frank, he went back to Boston and entered in his memo book, "Told MBG about LEM." MBG was of course his mother—and if she tried to add "no redhead" to her ukase about dwarfs, widows, et al., the memo book didn't say so. He also told Aunt Kit, who implied again that she didn't see what in the world he needed with a wife.

He also told them he was moving his head office to New York, and that meant they'd all move there. Martha did her best to smile, but the thought of breaking up their beautiful Boston home caused Kit to burst into tears.

CHAPTER 8

Lillian Worth a Billion

Now that she was engaged, Lillie became somewhat more interested in her wardrobe than she had been. Even so, she prevailed upon Grosie to do most of the trousseau-shopping, while she herself started to read a stack of books and magazines about construction work, in the Oakland Library.

She wrote that she was "astonished and rather humiliated to learn that there existed a whole body of literature . . . of which I knew not even the vocabulary."

She also started a notebook about what she had learned at the construction projects she had visited with Frank.

"It was fascinating to watch the stone mason's love of craft that led more than once to sacrifice the skin of finger rather than bruise his stone," she wrote. "The finger would grow a new skin but the stone, once injured, would stay spoiled forever."

The point is that while the conventional contractor would have been watching the stone and Frank would have been watching the mason's motions, Lillie was watching the mason's dedication to his job. And it was that emphasis on the *human* side of management that was to make the Gilbreth System unique.

Shortly after Frank returned to Boston, he mailed Lillie a copy of a confidential management booklet he had written for use within his own organization, which now numbered 8,000 to 10,000 men. The booklet was called *Field System,* and was largely responsible for the speed and efficiency of the Gilbreth organization. Frank guarded its contents so carefully that he numbered each copy, and required the bonding of his superintendents to whom copies were issued.

Despite these precautions, the booklet eventually got into the hands of his competitors. An article in the November 1907 issue of *Business World* said that one competitor constructed *Field System* piecemeal, from data obtained by bribing office boys and discharged superintendents.

Field System was written in 1902, and Lillie received her copy in 1904. The booklet is important today mainly for the light it casts on Frank's pioneering in scientific management and labor relations.

In those days, labor unions were just beginning to feel their own power, but there were few laws on the books to protect them from unscrupulous employers, who in the past had had a right to hire and fire at will.

One thorn in the flesh of the labor leaders was the infamous "blacklist" maintained by some industries, to prevent "agitators" and union members in general from getting jobs.

Frank went in the opposite direction. *Field System* established within the Gilbreth organization a "whitelist" of good performers, who would always be hired immediately on a

Gilbreth job, regardless of their union status. Whenever Frank landed a new contract, postcards went out to all "whitelist" men, telling them what jobs were available.

The booklet also showed how far Frank was ahead of his day in dealing with unions, because it spelled out not only his acceptance of, but his *preference* for, unions, within certain bounds. "Union laborers are to be given preference at all times," he wrote, "but no nonsense is to be taken from them . . . . Business agents of unions are to have full opportunity to consult job stewards. See they confine themselves strictly to business."

Frank's unprecedented policies to help employes improve themselves were also outlined for the first time. He told his superintendents that it was their *responsibility* to upgrade their men and see that they were happy.

"We want to find the highest task a man can perform permanently, year after year, and thrive and be happy," he wrote his superintendents in a separate memorandum. "A man wants to do more than get fat; he wants to be happy."

Field System also instructed superintendents to pay special attention to youngsters on the job. "Help apprentice boys in every way to learn and get promoted," Frank wrote. "Answer all their questions that are asked in good faith."

In the still nonexistent field of scientific management, the booklet stressed the importance of communications with employes. It also gave a *reason* for every rule promulgated. For instance:

—"Bills of lading must be obtained in duplicate, or we shall not be able to obtain credit for shipment."

—"Worn shovels should have handles sawed off so they cannot be used. Shovels cost 75 cents, and enough more work can be done in a short time with new shovels to pay for them."

"Acid is not to be taken into the lockers. The fumes will destroy ropes and cause accidents."

Frank also opened lines of communications through what was to become the Suggestions Box. "We shall appreciate and pay money for suggestions that will improve this system," he wrote. "Suggestions lead to promotion and increased value. They show a capacity for greater responsibilities. Write your suggestion and mail it to F.B.G., marked personal."

Finally, *Field System* plowed new ground by directing that progress pictures be taken on all jobs; by outlining a unique method of on-the-job accounting which required no books; and by explaining a new type of cost-plus contract to be used exclusively on all Gilbreth jobs.

Although the cost-plus procedure is probably as old as contracting itself, Frank formalized and popularized it, and he alone, among the big contractors, would use no other procedure. *Field System* spelled out the specifics which are employed to this day by the United States government in cost-plus defense contracts.

There was also one other detail which, although far from earth-shaking, indicated Frank's thoroughness. He wrote that the telephone on each project should be located at a place where the boss who was using it could also keep an eye on how the work was going, while he waited for "Central" to answer.

Lillie read and reread the booklet, and was astute enough to see—or at any rate to suspect—that Frank's *system* was even more important than his building business. She wrote him a note saying so, and subsequently recorded in *The Quest of the One Best Way* that Frank "was persuaded to enter more thoroughly and seriously into the task of reducing all methods to writing, which was to become, if that were possible, of literary as well as scientific value."

As a surprise to Frank, Lillie indexed *Field System,* and this was incorporated in later editions of the volume. Frank thought it was wonderful that his wife-to-be was so interested in his work, and wrote her that if she was a good girl he might allow her to index *all* the books he intended to author.

"Do you remember what Thoreau said after he had written his first book—and nobody had paid any attention to it?" Frank added. "He said, 'I now have a library of 1,000 books, 998 of which I wrote myself.' Something like that. Anyway, that's F.B.G."

During their engagement, they also decided that the slogan for the Gilbreth System which they hoped to devise would be "The One Best Way to Do Work."

"Of course, ours was also to be a One Best Marriage," Lillie wrote in *The Quest.* "The Mrs. Gilbreth-to-be was encouraged to find that she was considered not only a possible but a promising pupil."

The wedding took place October 19, 1904, at the Mollers' home in Oakland, and Papa wept as he gave away his Firefly. They spent the night in the bridal suite of the St. Francis Hotel in San Francisco, where the next morning the waiter spilled the overloaded breakfast tray onto the bed and part of Lillie's trousseau. The bride was too embarrassed to say much, but the groom gave the waiter a lecture on the inefficiencies of a "lazy man's load." On Frank's construction projects, a "lazy man's load" was defined as one too cumbersome or heavy to be handled safely in one trip, and workmen were cautioned to make two trips instead. The waiter cleaned up the mess and brought a new breakfast, this time dividing the load.

They took a Pullman east, and Lillie wasn't too pleased to discover that two aging friends of her parents had the section next to theirs. But Frank welcomed the company and, being practically a commuter on transcontinental trains, helped arrange the luggage of the older people, and made certain that George, the porter, gave them good service.

Sometime during the trip, Frank and Lillie made a pact that they'd have an even dozen children. Six boys and six girls would be just about right, Frank said. That's the way it turned out, too. But even after the twelfth arrived, Frank used to pretend that Lillie was an underachiever when it came to motherhood. "But never mind, Lillie," he'd say with mock condolence, "you did the best you could."

Honeymooners on Pullmans have always been deemed comic figures, but Frank didn't care. Sometimes, when he felt too many eyes were on him and Lillie, he'd adopt a professorial tone and make believe he was teaching her about his work.

"When it comes to concrete," he'd say, "the basic materials are cement and sand. When properly mixed—but let me illustrate, and please pay close attention."

Then, while she'd lean over his shoulder and try to shield what he was doing, he'd draw outrageous caricatures of the people who were surreptitiously watching them—with arrows pointing to the various subjects. Sometimes Lillie couldn't help but titter, and the onlookers probably deduced that the honeymooners didn't spend *all* their time talking about concrete.

Lillie certainly spent part of *her* time wondering what life would be like in New York with the "duplicate mothers." Martha and Kit had already moved, with their own furniture, into the apartment at Riverside Drive and Ninety-fourth Street. Every time Lillie thought of the two women sitting sharp-eyed and straight-backed in their identical rockers, poised to wait on Frank hand and foot, she felt depressed and downright frightened.

But of course she didn't mention that to Frank, and it simply wasn't in her nature to complain. So, instead, Lillie put her mind on how to make theirs the "One Best Marriage." And as the train sped eastward, the two future management engineers planned their merger with painstaking detail.

In *The Quest* and later in *Living with Our Children,* Lillie looked back with nostalgia and amusement on the analytical approach of the newlyweds to their "One Best Marriage." But, at the same time, she recommended a similar approach for all young couples.

"It started with a survey of qualifications and aptitudes . . . which were amusing even to the two people involved," Lillie wrote, "but which proved of great service. The 'One Best Marriage' was to be secured through analyzing other successful marriages and synthesizing the result into a plan for this one. . . .

"Does this seem too much like an engineering project? It did not to us. . . . It did not remove romance or interest, but added a stability and a long view."

They made lists of the things they thought they could do well, in order to "see what each might contribute to the new partnership."

Then they made lists of things that irritated them and things that they liked—both "rational and irrational." Frank found some of the results downright disconcerting.

"You have red hair and I had always resolved I would marry a brunette," Lillie quoted him as saying. "You are tall, and I admire short girls."

"Red hair often stands for activity, and there are sometimes advantages in being tall," Lillie countered. "So there you are."

And, finally, each partner jotted down what he could remember of his family history, so they could appraise whatever endowment they might have to hand down to their children.

Their conclusion in this regard was that, if they failed to do a good job of bringing up the dozen children who were on the drawing board, they would have "no right to use heredity as an excuse for failure."

In other words, it would simply be up to them to provide the proper environment and education.

Lillie-the-psychologist may have had her own dealings with Martha and Kit in mind when she wrote in *Living with Our Children* that the lists of likes, dislikes, and ancestors are valuable in cementing relations with in-laws.

"Many a friendly mother-in-law—and there are more of these than the world lets us know—has herself furnished the young wife with a list of her husband's likes," she said.

"Many a dear grandmother or aunt finds her own passion for genealogy shared at last, when given her first opportunity to expand on the achievements of the family—and gets the satisfaction of making the things she loves best of service to the people she loves most.

"Two warnings: Neither partner can act on the assumption that because the other likes something in another man or woman it will be acceptable in him or her. Many a bride remembers the day when she went to the beauty parlor to be made to look as nearly as possible like someone her husband admired, and went home to be greeted, not with praise, but with a horror-stricken, 'You're a fright. Fix yourself the way you were!' Nor can either expect that likes and dislikes will not change with the circumstances. But that is what makes life interesting."

When they had at last completed their marriage analysis,

Frank pretended to have some second thoughts about at least one of the lists he had made out.

"Maybe you'd better tear up that list about my dislikes," he said. "I'm beginning to realize I may have made a horrible mistake. How could a husband be so stupid as to deliver into his wife's hands a written recipe of exactly how to run him crazy?"

"Don't worry about that," Lillie smiled. "That's something that all we red-haired women know how to do by instinct, without any recipe."

As the train passed through various cities, Frank would often point out buildings he had constructed. And he shocked Lillie and her parents' friends with some tall stories about the wild and woolly conditions he had encountered in some of the cow towns.

"There's a saloon in this burg," he'd say with a straight face, "that's mighty tough. A tenderfoot once walked into it, bellied up to the bar, and asked the bartender: 'Where did you get grapes out here this time of year?'

" 'Grapes?' said the bartender. 'Where do you see any grapes? '

" 'All over the floor,' said the tenderfoot.

" 'Oh, those ain't grapes, mister! I ain't had a chance to sweep the place out yet. Those are eyes that were gouged out last night.' "

They stopped at St. Louis to see the World's Fair, but they had hardly arrived when Frank received a telegram from his home office saying that some sort of a crisis had occurred—so they took the next train to New York. In the shuffle, Lillie's baggage was lost—and she arrived at the apartment with the clothes she had on her back, and a single suitcase containing an assortment of apparel, some of which still bore faint stains from the breakfast-tray accident in San Francisco.

Somehow or other, the two older women and Lillie worked out their design for living. But it must have been difficult for all of them—and particularly for Lillie, who often felt useless and untalented when compared to her new in-laws.

Having grown up in a house full of servants, Lillie couldn't cook or sew, and didn't have the slightest idea about how to market or run a house. And on all of those matters, Martha, the ex-boardinghouse matron, was practically the world's champion.

Lillie liked to paint and sketch, and Kit was an accomplished artist. Lillie liked to play the piano, and Sister Anne, a frequent visitor, was a professional.

When Lillie and Frank first arrived at the apartment, dinner was ready, and the duplicate mothers had prepared all of Frank's favorite dishes in quantities large enough to, well, choke a horse.

Frank never liked to serve—and as already noted was usually late to meals—so Martha had always presided at the head of the table. But now Martha escorted Lillie to the head position. When Lillie discovered that this meant carving the meat and "helping" the plates—and when she saw how ill at ease Martha was—she got up and invited her mother-in-law to resume her normal place.

"You see," Lillie once told us, explaining how she first got to know Martha, "it was really much more *efficient* that way. So don't think you ought to feel sorry for me. It all worked out very nicely."

Still, the shy, sensitive Firefly—who had become deathly sick the last time she tried to live in New York—had a fairly hellish year of it, judging from all accounts.

When her wedding presents and some beautiful furniture arrived from the West Coast, there simply wasn't any room for them, and she had to put most of them in storage.

Kit, who once had been a charming person, had developed diabetes—and hadn't told anybody about it. The result was that she was extremely irritable, and while she managed to put on a cheerful front when Frank was around, she was often disagreeable to both Lillie and Martha when he was gone.

As for Martha herself, although she was tactless and terribly outspoken, no one had a kinder heart—so she tried very hard indeed to make Lillie feel at home. But of course Lillie should have *been* at home and Martha should have *felt* at home. As a result, the atmosphere was often strained.

"I love to *visit* Aunt Martha," one Bunker kinsman confided sympathetically to Lillie after coming to tea, "but I wouldn't want to live in the same house with her if you paid me—especially as her daughter-in-law."

"Why she's a *lovely* person!" Lillie objected loyally.

"Of course she is! But that's not the point," was the unanswerable reply.

So when Lillie told us that it "all worked out very nicely," what she meant was that it worked out very nicely long range. Poor Kit finally went to a doctor, but it was too late then for him to do anything for her, and she died shortly thereafter. Kit's death brought Lillie and Martha closer together, and they grew to love and respect each other—again, long range.

But short range? Frank was on the road much of the time, going from one building project to another. There wasn't a bit of housework to do; the two older women monopolized that department. Lillie visited Papa's sisters every so often, but they had their own friends. She passed some of the days alone on a houseboat Frank had acquired, which was anchored in the Hudson. And at night she studied engineering publications and mulled over files which Frank had carted home from his office, so that his bride could become familiar with his work.

More and more, Lillie became convinced that the Gilbreth System could offer something infinitely more important to the world than the Gilbreth buildings. But she decided she wouldn't say any more about that until she became familiar with the whole picture.

When Frank was on the road, they'd write every day, and often he'd send her silly poetry like:

> Here's to Lillian
> Worth a billion
> To an officer or civilian.
>
> Her epitaph
> (It's not to laugh)
> My absolutely perfect half.

On the nights that Frank was home, they often worked on two new books that Lillie said were needed to expand the Gilbreth System—to put into writing methods which already were in practice on Frank's jobs. These books, *Concrete System* and *Bricklaying System,* eventually were published in 1908 and 1909, respectively.

When Lillie looked back on those early days in New York, it was the happy times working on those books—rather than the lonesome days when Frank was away—that she chose to remember.

"Never were evenings set aside or engagements kept so carefully for the opera, theater or other pleasures as were the evenings to review the bond [concrete] charts, first as rough sketches and later as galley and as finished page proof," she wrote. "Never was box of candy or flowers received with such enthusiasm as the large rolls [charts] that the young builder brought home in the evening. . . . Never was any work undertaken with more joy or proved a greater satisfaction from start to finish."

And as they worked together, it became increasingly plain to both of them that "scientific management" meant more than machines, accounting procedures, and inventory control. It meant, first of all, the *people* who did the jobs. As Lillie put it in *The Quest:*

"Unconsciously to Frank, more or less, there was coming into his work the systematic and finally the scientific handling of the human element, which is really so much more important in getting the results desired."

Meanwhile, Frank's contracting business kept growing, and he was traveling up to 60,000 miles a year. Lillie started accompanying him on a good many trips, and would go with him to his building projects during the day, and work with him at nights on the slowly evolving Gilbreth System. Finally Lillie became as adept and fearless as he at climbing over high scaffolds and balancing along concrete walls.

One of Frank's favorite stunts was to arrive unannounced at a construction project, dressed city-slicker fashion and with Lillie on his arm, and go directly to the bricklayers. There, he'd make loud remarks about how easy bricklaying seemed. Finally, one of the men would rise to the bait, and tell him that if it seemed so easy maybe he'd like to try it. So, after considerable urging either to try it or shut up, he'd remove his coat with a show of reluctance. Then, after taking off his tie and detachable collar, which he'd hand to Lillie, he'd take a trowel and give it a double flip in the air, to test its weight. And with that, bricks and mortar would start to fly. His hands might be soft and his nails manicured, but he hadn't forgotten the technique.

Then usually one of his "whitelist" workers—the top-notch men who had been on Gilbreth jobs before and had preference—would wander up, recognize him, and holler: "By God, it's the boss himself—nobody else can lay bricks like *that!* I hope you guys didn't *bet* him."

They'd shake hands all around, and by that time the superintendent would usually appear to see who was disturbing his workmen and causing a crowd to gather. So Frank would clean his hands on a rag, and put on his collar, tie, and coat, and he, Lillie, and the super would go to the project office and get down to business.

Lillie was subjected to that bricklaying act a good many times, but if it ever embarrassed her or she grew tired of it, she never mentioned it. Even when Frank first came to call at her house in Oakland, before they were married, he had gone into the act to "entertain" an unsuspecting workman who was repairing the bricks in a fireplace.

But the traveling was tiring for both of them, even though they did enjoy the train rides together, which gave them time to work on their system.

And then the children started arriving. And arriving. And arriving.

CHAPTER 9

Master Builder

Lillie never had much trouble with her confinements, and prided herself on keeping them as brief and efficient as possible. She elected to have all the births at home, with the exception of her youngest, Jane.

"Well, after eleven of them, I thought I was *entitled* to the luxury of a good rest in the hospital," Lillie used to explain about Jane.

Even though Frank eventually became mighty experienced in the role of expectant father, he always became terribly nervous as the actual delivery approached. In traditional fashion, he'd pace endlessly and go out into the kitchen to supervise the boiling of huge tubs of water. The water was rarely used, but the general practitioners of the day always liked to have plenty on hand, partly because the supervision of the boiling managed to get fidgety fathers out of the way.

Some of his nervousness would rub off on us children, who sometimes would fall in behind him and pace too—which made him all the more nervous. And we'd all give a big cheer of relief and go around shaking each other's hands when the first wail of the newborn baby was heard.

A few minutes later, Grandma would come out, followed by the doctor, and let us know whether it was a boy or a girl. And not too long after that, we'd all be allowed to go in and see Mother and the new baby together. That's when we all thought that Mother looked her most beautiful—although you could hardly say the same for a newborn baby—and Dad looked his most proud.

During those first years of the "One Best Marriage," the family moved from New York to San Francisco, back to New York again, and then to Plainfield, New Jersey.

By that time, Frank had perfected his "cost plus a fixed sum" method of doing business—the only way he'd bid for a construction job. He ran double-page advertisements in newspapers and magazines listing all the advantages of "cost plus" on one page, and leaving the other blank except for one "disadvantage": That if your contractor made a mistake and bid too low, you couldn't get your building at less than cost. Some people thought he went too far in espousing his one method and called him a "preacher."

The move to San Francisco was prompted by the earthquake of 1906, and the large number of rebuilding jobs that were available. A week after the earthquake, Gilbreth ran a sixteen-page ad in the *Engineering Record* saying he was ready to rebuild the city. When he arrived in San Francisco, he bought a Pierce Arrow car and hired a publicity man for $40 a week. Reporters trailed after him when he visited the charred ruins to learn what he could about safety factors. He pointed out to them that wood and brick were on the way out, and that his new buildings would be of concrete and steel.

As he picked up contract after contract, he instructed his New York office to send materials by carload lots, because he couldn't risk the delays that smaller shipments were experiencing.

"Mark them, 'GIVE THIS CAR RIGHT OF WAY, Frank B. Gilbreth, General Contractor,' " he ordered.

When his home office manager wired that if Frank kept up the pace he might overload that office, Gilbreth replied, "You bet your last dollar I will! Why the hell won't I? That's exactly what I've been trying to do all my life. I shall land thirty million dollars' worth in the next twenty-four months. Get Ready For It!"

He built the largest pulpwood plant in the country at Canton, North Carolina; the St. Croix Paper Company's plant and town at Spragues Falls, Maine; the industrial town of Piercefield, New York; and apartment houses, factories, and hospitals in almost every city in the country. The panic of 1907 almost put him out of business, but by 1909 he was going strong again, and wrote in his diary that he had more contracts than ever before.

The main fly in the ointment was that Frank was having to spend more and more time in courts around the country. Even to this day, no Gilbreth building has ever had a structural failure, so there were no suits on that. But the basic trouble with Frank's cost-plus system, then as now, is disagreement as to what constitutes actual cost. And since he always insisted on sticking to his guns rather than settling, he found himself involved in a good deal of litigation. Also, he usually had more than a score of other suits pending against competitors who infringed on his various patents.

Lillie, who always detested fights and arguments, thought

that every minute he spent in the courtroom was a waste of talent; and Frank couldn't disagree.

Lillie realized it would be terribly difficult to tell a man who had started as a bricklayer and become a master builder that he ought to fold up his business and go into something that might not even pay him a bare living. But she was becoming convinced that the Gilbreth System, properly applied, might literally make living easier for people around the world.

"Frank is only beginning to realize and use his highest capabilities," she wrote her mother.

And she resolved to herself that she'd get him out of the courtrooms and off the building scaffolds—and that together they'd expand the system for the benefit of people everywhere.

There were three daughters—Anne, Mary, and Ernestine —in the family when Frank, Lillie, and Martha moved to Plainfield, New Jersey, in 1909. The town is within easy commuting distance of New York, and Lillie preferred rearing her children in a spacious suburban house rather than a Manhattan apartment.

When a fourth daughter, Martha, was born that same year, Frank began to get impatient for a son. But he tried to be a good sport about it. He kept telling Lillie that if she wanted to stay in the same old groove and continue producing daughters—even though some people *did* think that variety was the spice of life—that certainly was her prerogative. And he added that if she wanted to change her mind and aim for a dozen daughters—instead of the half-and-half arrangement they *definitely* had agreed on—he supposed that was a woman's privilege.

Lillie must have got the hint, however subtle, for her fifth baby was a boy, named for his father. Frank was so jubilant that the doctor wanted to give him a sedative, and Martha threatened to throw a bucket of cold water on him if he didn't stop grabbing her hands and making her jump up and down with him, ring-around-the-rosy fashion. When Lillie eventually saw the telephone and telegraph bills, she accused him of having relayed the glad tidings to all relatives down to and including third cousins, and casual acquaintances as well.

Meanwhile, Lillie and Frank had both been working on various phases of scientific management. The year they moved to Plainfield, Frank had finally found a publisher for *Bricklaying System,* on which they had worked when they first lived in New York.

In this book, they spelled out for the first time Frank's original experiments designed to speed bricklaying—what he called Motion Study. And they said in so many words that Motion Study should be applied to *all* industry, and that workmen as well as the bosses should share the inevitable benefits.

"The Motion Study in this book is but the beginning of an *era* of Motion Study," *Bricklaying System* said. "It will cut down production costs and increase the efficiency and wages of the workman."

The book went on to say that workmen on Gilbreth construction jobs who even so much as *tried* to utilize his Motion Study methods would get bonuses, and that those who tried and were successful would get substantial pay increases and would go home happier each day, because they'd be less tired.

The book bore only Frank's name, because to have listed a woman as a collaborator would have been the kiss of death.

But Frank made it plain, in correspondence and in speeches, that Lillie was his partner.

As for Lillie, she was hard at work on a thesis which she hoped would be accepted for a doctorate at the University of California. She had been assured—or at least she thought she had—that the thesis would be considered by the university, and that the normal requirement of attending classes there would be waived, since all the field work was being done in the East.

She called her opus *The Psychology of Management,* and it eventually became the keystone of her contributions to that field, and the credentials which admitted her to the hitherto all-male circle of engineering.

The thesis made it plain that scientific management should be aimed, primarily, at happiness and abundance for *all* people.

"The emphasis in successful management lies on the man, not on the work," she wrote. "Efficiency is best secured by . . . modifying the equipment, materials, and methods to make the most of the man."

Then she added that "with knowledge will come ability to understand the rights of others" and that this would "lead the way to that true Brotherhood which may some day come to be."

The so-called robber barons of the day would certainly have taken a dim view of that! But they didn't get a chance to see it, right away, because when Lillie submitted *The Psychology of Management* to the University of California, she was informed that there had been a misunderstanding. The university officials explained that the thesis couldn't be accepted, and she couldn't be awarded her Ph.D., without at least a year of residency.

Lillie was crushed of course, but she had developed a positive philosophy and knew in her heart that, even if she didn't get a doctorate, the time spent on the thesis had been anything but wasted.

However, Frank, who had no such philosophy to fall back on, was simply furious. And when Lillie tried to tell him that it would all eventually work out all right, he maintained, though with grudging admiration, that she made Pollyanna look like a surly grouch.

"Your own alma mater!" he bellowed. "They don't have a decent course out there in psychology, and they don't have any course at all in management—and yet you have to go to classes out there for a year or two so they can teach you about them."

Actually, California had some excellent courses in psychology, and Frank probably knew it. He was certainly correct, though, about not having any in management.

Right on the heels of that disappointment came an eleven-month nightmare. One of the daughters came down with diphtheria and almost died. She eventually recovered, and everyone breathed a sigh of relief. But then Mary, the next-to-oldest, was stricken and in two weeks she was dead.

Frank was so overcome with grief that he simply couldn't cope with things, and went into a shell. For days he didn't go to work or want to talk with anyone. Then the two other girls came down with it and almost died. After they had recovered, I came down with it.

Neither Frank nor Lillie ever discussed Mary again, at least in the presence of us children. And for years thereafter, if one of the younger children asked Mother about Mary, she'd do her best to answer calmly, and then retire hastily to her room, with her shoulders shaking in sobs.

Still, Lillie's philosophy enabled her to write in *The Quest,* "In spite of the fact that diphtheria had wrought such havoc, the family came through in excellent health, ready to undertake new difficulties or rejoice in new achievements."

No account of the birth of scientific management can dodge the bitter and sometimes heartbreaking encounters between the Gilbreth and Taylor systems. And while a Gilbreth may not be deemed an ideal narrator of this unpleasantness—any more than would a Hatfield of the McCoy feud—it can't be dodged here.

Frederick W. Taylor, generally recognized as the "father of scientific management," was ten years older than Frank. As early as 1895, when Frank was just going into business for himself, Taylor was telling factory managers they could speed production by applying scientific methods.

Taylor soon became known as a man who could stop "soldiering on the job." He accomplished this by piecework and what he described as Time Study.

Piecework, a pay scale based on actual production rather than work-hours, dates back to ancient days. But Taylor was the first to analyze and time each job, show the worker a more efficient way to perform it, and then base piecework pay scales on his Time Study.

The net result was increased production for the factory and, theoretically, higher pay for the worker—although some unscrupulous employers promptly lowered the pay scales as soon as the pieceworkers became more productive.

Frank used to tell about trying to help improve the motions of one girl on piecework, only to find her utterly discouraged. "What's the use," she told him. "The boss here cuts the piecerate when any girl earns over $6 a week."

In 1903, the year after Frank wrote *Field System,* Taylor presented his famous *Paper 1003,* entitled *Shop Management,* to the American Society of Mechanical Engineers

(A.S.M.E.). And scientific management—although it still wasn't known by that name—was born.

Field System was, of course, only a work manual for Gilbreth projects. *Shop Management* covered the whole scope of industry, and was the first public presentation of how scientific methods could speed production.

Taylor's paper made a worldwide impact that seems incredible today. The general public saw in the Taylor System something that could raise everyone's standard of living. Congressional hearings were held on whether utility rates and railroad fares could be reduced if the Taylor System were applied.

Prior to the publication of *Shop Management,* there was virtually no literature on how to manage a factory. Apprentices learned from journeymen, assistant foremen from foremen, and assistant managers from managers. But now a managerial plan had been spelled out which the public thought might mean prosperity for all.

If there were any Doubting Thomases among engineers, Taylor convinced them by his experiments with a now immortal steelworker named Schmidt. When Taylor started to study Schmidt, that worthy was shoveling pig iron at a rate of twelve tons a day. Taylor showed him how he could shovel forty-seven.

Taylor unquestionably was a genius, but he seemed to have what amounted almost to contempt for workers. To keep them from striking, he was willing to pay them more for their increased production. But he was a management man and he believed management should keep the lion's share.

Taylor showed his Achilles' heel when he wrote, in connection with his Schmidt experiments, that the first requirement of a pig-iron shoveler "is that he shall be so stupid and phlegmatic that he more nearly resembles an ox than any other type."

A basic difference between the Taylor System and the subsequent Gilbreth System was this almost contemptuous attitude. While Taylor was writing that a worker must not be allowed to "produce any longer by his own initiative, but should execute punctiliously the orders given," the Gilbreths were establishing a Suggestions Box.

And instead of viewing employes as so many oxen, the Gilbreths viewed them as human beings who had a right to happiness. Frank and Lillie maintained that it was the *duty* of owners and managers to make their employes happy, and that the amount of happiness each person created was a measure of his own life.

In fact, the closing paragraph of the Gilbreths' book *Fatigue Study,* written in 1915, told the factory owners something they had never heard before—and it dramatizes the difference between the two systems.

"The good of your life," *Fatigue Study* concluded, "consists of the quantity of 'Happiness Minutes' that you have created or caused. Increase your own record by eliminating unnecessary fatigue of the workers!"

In spite of Taylor's views about workingmen, his system changed the course of industry. And when Frank read *Shop Management* in 1903 he called it a work of genius. But Lillie wasn't so sure—and she could never forget the reference to the ox.

Frank first met Taylor in December 1907 in the lobby of the Engineering Societies Building in New York. Thereafter, at least until the feud erupted, Frank would sometimes point to a corner of the lobby and remark in awed tones,

"Here on this spot I met the only man who has brought a message to the world in the last twenty-five years."

Gilbreth and Taylor became great friends—or so Frank thought—but Taylor was so shy and introverted that no one ever got very close to him. By then, Taylor was espousing his system almost as if it were a holy cause. He was so dedicated that he refused to accept money for management consultation. Instead, he surrounded himself with a small group, known as his "disciples," who could be hired individually by industries to install "Dr. Taylor's System."

Taylor was too reserved to make a very effective public speaker, but Frank was developing into a true platform artist. Although still a contractor, Frank had reached engineering status, and was a member of the A.S.M.E. During the time that the family lived in Plainfield, he became in great demand on the college lecture circuit.

Recognizing this, Taylor asked Frank to explain the Taylor System in his college talks. When Frank agreed, and did a fine job of it, Taylor asked him to explain the system to the New York Civic Forum and the Western Economic Society. The result in both cases was wide newspaper coverage.

Taylor was grateful and even told his disciples that "Gilbreth has done our cause a very fine service." Although he didn't elevate Frank to disciple rank, he conferred on both Frank and Lillie the next best thing: a standing invitation to his home near Philadelphia, where he sometimes held court for his disciples and others. The home was known as Boxly, and Lillie wrote in *The Quest:*

"The company assembled in the early morning, in the beautiful, large living room at Boxly, to be greeted by Taylor and often his two young sons. Pads of paper and pencils were distributed, as Taylor very much objected to interruption. The lecture lasted from two hours on, then followed the time of questions, then luncheon. . . . Practically the same lecture seemed to be given each time, and it was also the lecture that Taylor gave when he spoke away from home."

Perhaps Taylor was testing Frank's mettle, to determine whether he was of disciple material. But in any event, Lillie was confronted with a real dilemma: She wanted Frank to get out of the contracting business and become a management consultant so that they could espouse the Gilbreth System. But since Taylor was running what amounted to a closed shop, the only way to become a management consultant was to espouse the Taylor System. And she wondered whether Frank could *ever* help install a system—however meritorious—in which some workers were thought of as cattle.

The Taylor System was such an amazing breakthrough, however, that Frank couldn't lose sight of its importance, and he pointed out that Taylor himself had said repeatedly workers should benefit from it. Actually, Frank maintained during the years the family lived in Plainfield that the whole new science should forever be known as the Taylor System, in tribute to its originator, rather than scientific managment. The latter term didn't even come into wide use until 1910, when it was adopted informally by a group of ten advocates of Taylor's principles, who had been called together by Louis D. Brandeis. The ten, including Frank, had agreed to testify, at a rate hearing by the Interstate Commerce Commission, that the railroads could save millions of dollars by applying the Taylor System. Brandeis, who subsequently became a Supreme Court justice, was representing the Trade Association of the Atlantic Seaboard. He hoped to convince the I.C.C. that the railroads could increase their profits by making economies, and thus shouldn't be allowed to raise rates.

Prior to the hearing, Brandeis urged his ten witnesses to agree on exactly what they would call the new science in their testimony. Among the names suggested were "Taylor System," "industrial management," and "scientific management." Frank voted for "Taylor System," but the majority favored "scientific management," and that term soon became used universally.

The rate increase eventually was denied. Meanwhile, Frank had an opportunity to talk at length with Brandeis, who was his close friend and was all but idolized by organized labor because of championing the constitutionality of state wage-and-hour laws. Frank urged him to "show the workers of this country that we are trying to help them, and thus allay their unwarranted suspicions of what we've now agreed to call scientific management."

As still another tribute to Taylor, Frank called together a group of engineers November 9, 1910, at the New York Athletic Club, and founded a society to promote the Taylor System. He wanted to call the new organization the Taylor Society, but he was outvoted, and it was named the Society to Promote the Science of Management. After Taylor's death, though, the organization's name was changed to the Taylor Society.

But even though Taylor appreciated all Frank had done for him, he would scarcely listen when Frank tried to tell him about the system that he and Lillie had been working on, which stressed the elimination of unnecessary motions and fatigue, rather than speed against the clock. And when Frank showed Taylor copies of *Field System* and *Concrete System,* he reported that Taylor seemed "hurt and distant."

Still, Frank and Lillie kept working on Motion Study, and

then scored a major breakthrough of their own: the first use of the moving picture camera to record the motions of workers.

Hitherto, all studies of motions had been guesswork, and involved either hidden stopwatches in the pockets of management men, or asking a worker openly to go through his work cycle, over and over again. Either procedure was not only inexact, but was apt to cause disruption in union-minded plants.

Frank could invite a single worker into his moving picture laboratory, and have the worker go through his motions one time. The worker was photographed against a background of four-inch squares, so that Frank could see the exact path of each motion. Also in the background was a large clock which rotated even faster than a stopwatch. Inscribed on its face, in letters not quite so large as a house, was the name "Gilbreth."

The Gilbreths called this new technique "micromotion study," and Frank always considered it his most important contribution to scientific management, because it could be used in scores of different fields, ranging from surgery to the loading of a machine gun.

Now Frank and Lillie could run a film over and over again, to determine exactly why one bricklayer could produce faster than another. They could stop the film, back it up, or run it in slow motion. Now they could study the motions of a drill-press operator, and redesign the machine so that it could be operated faster, more safely, and with less fatigue. Now special posture chairs could be designed at a height which fit the operator's motions, so that he could get off his feet and be less tired at the end of the day.

Again, when Frank tried to tell Taylor about micromotion study, Taylor called it trivia and said it was all a part of Time Study, anyway. Frank noted in his diary: "He said it was undoubtedly good where one was investigating the minutia of motions. He acted so that I saw he was hurt and so I changed the subject."

But if Frank had hurt Taylor's feelings, Taylor reciprocated when he published his now-famous *The Principles of Scientific Management* in February 1911—a few months before the diphtheria epidemic at Plainfield.

The first edition of this book was printed privately and distributed only to members of the A.S.M.E. One paragraph said, "For more than thirty years, time and motion study men . . . have been devoting their whole time to scientific motion study followed by accurate time study."

That was bad enough, because it dated motion study at a time when Frank was thirteen years old, and Lillie was three.

In the autumn of 1911, Taylor brought out a second edition for the general public, published by Harper, and for some reason he had added a paragraph saying that his No. 1 disciple, Sanford Thompson, was "perhaps the most experienced man in motion study" in the United States. Incidentally, Thompson himself eventually denied this, but not until both Taylor and Frank were dead. The denial said that, "as to motion study per se, in my opinion it was original with Mr. Gilbreth."

The disappointment about Lillie's doctorate, the diphtheria epidemic, and Taylor's calculated downgrading of Frank's Motion Study efforts all added up to two disastrous years.

When the epidemic finally was over and the Master

Builder went back full-time to his contracting business, some of the enthusiasm seemed to have drained out of him. As for Lillie, Plainfield had so many tragic and unpleasant memories that she knew she could never be happy there again.

CHAPTER 10

Back to College

When Lillie had to make up her mind on something important, she relied on a method she said was devised by Benjamin Franklin. She'd list the pros and the cons in parallel columns—not unlike the advertisements that Frank used to run for his cost-plus system—and then add them up.

"This seemed the One Best Way to attack the problem" of whether they should become management engineers, she wrote in *The Quest*.

By now, Frank had regained his enthusiasm and verve. They sat at the dining room table of their Plainfield house, one night after Martha and the children had gone to bed, and Lillie drew the parallel columns on a piece of typewriting paper.

"All right, what's the first point?" Frank asked.

"We both know what *that* is," replied Lillie, wrinkling her brow. "Can we make a living at it?"

Frank knew how upset she still was over the loss of Mary, and he was determined to cheer her up and keep the conversation light.

"Don't worry about that, Boss," he chuckled. "You know very well I could swim mother-naked up to Manhattan Island, and if somebody would give me two copies of the day's paper I'd make a suit out of one, sell the other, and be in business."

"So that goes in the plus column," Lillie smiled.

"The only trouble is," Frank conceded, "that if I put on any more weight I might have to use *both* papers for that suit."

"Cheer up, dear," said Pollyana, who certainly was shrewd enough to realize that was precisely what Frank was trying to get *her* to do, "maybe it'll be Sunday, and the papers will be extra large."

"Anyway," Frank continued, "I guess the next point is whether the Gilbreth System is *ready* to be installed in a factory. We think so, but probably no one else does. So how are you going to list that, Dr. Franklin?"

"It's a pro and a con—it goes in both columns. The next question is what do we really *want* to do?"

"Another pro," Frank nodded.

As the notations in the pro column lengthened, they made up their minds that Frank would start job-hunting the very next morning for a factory where he could install new methods to speed production.

"There was a growing realization that their best work lay in the field of handling the human element," Lillie wrote, "and that management engineering was bound to rise in importance and dignity. Added to this, there existed a passionate desire to succeed and an appetite for the job. And it was always a joy to work together!"

Since Frank knew that no factory-owner would risk trying an unknown plan like the Gilbreth System, he decided on a different approach: He'd offer to install the Taylor System for a fee, and as a dividend would make micromotion studies at his own expense.

Two months later, and after having talked with scores of factory-owners, he landed a job at the New England Butt Company in Providence, where his sister Anne lived. The Butt Company manufactured braiding machines for shoelaces and wire insulation, and was one of the leading firms in that specialized field.

"There's only one little, minor detail," Frank told Lillie, after he had broken the news. "I haven't cleared it with Dr. Taylor yet. And we don't get the job at all unless I can assure them Taylor approves."

Despite their differences and mutually hurt feelings, Frank and Taylor had retained a rapport, and Frank had continued his speeches in support of the Taylor System. So he didn't feel any embarrassment about approaching Taylor.

Frank began the conversation by telling Taylor about a book on Motion Study that he and Lillie planned to write. Frank was nonplussed when Taylor suddenly became enthusiastic about the project, and said that he and Thompson would collaborate with Frank and Lillie on the opus.

Frank thought, probably correctly, that this was a virtual offer of discipleship. So he postponed asking for approval of his job at the New England Butt Company until he could talk over this new development with Lillie.

Discipleship would have meant instant success for Frank

as a management engineer, with automatic approval of the Butt Company job, and subsequently more consulting jobs than he could handle.

"This seemed a most flattering and in many ways desirable offer," Lillie wrote in *The Quest,* "but Frank and his wife finally decided they preferred to issue their book alone, because it embodied their viewpoints and their aspirations. This was a most serious decision, because it meant they had decided to go it alone."

So Frank had the unpleasant task of returning to Taylor, rejecting with thanks his offer to collaborate, and then asking him to approve the job at the Butt Company.

Perhaps Taylor figured he owed Frank a favor for all those speeches he had made. Or perhaps Taylor thought it would be preferable for Frank to be installing the Taylor System than working on the Gilbreth System. Or perhaps Frank forgot to mention that he intended to make micromotion studies at the factory. Also, when the Taylor-Gilbreth feud is viewed in retrospect, it appears that most of the bad blood was between Gilbreth and Taylor's disciples, not Taylor himself.

At any rate, Taylor agreed to let Frank tackle the project, provided Frank would employ Taylor lieutenants who would report back directly to Taylor himself as to how the work was progressing.

So the contracts were signed, and, although the New England Butt Company didn't want Frank to start the project for close to a year, pending some sort of a reorganization, he and Lillie decided to leave Plainfield and its unhappy memories at once, and move to Providence.

Lillie had tried to like New York—"although of course it isn't San Francisco, dear," she used to say—and she had tried to make the best of Plainfield. But she simply loved Providence. And she was expecting another baby.

The family moved into a rambling house on Brown Street, just a block from the Brown University campus. And even while Lillie was arranging the furniture, Frank hastened to see some of his academic friends there about her enrolling for her Ph.D.

But when he came home bearing good news, Lillie wasn't so sure she should leave the children while she attended classes.

"Don't worry, Boss," Frank told her. "You can see our house from the classrooms. If you see one of our girls climbing out a window, you can run home and catch her before she hits the ground."

So Lillie became a co-ed, and everything started to go right again. Yes, she loved Providence and she loved Brown.

"Oh, the dignity and repose of the College on the Hill," she wrote. "The beautiful elms under which John Marshall, John Hay and Charles Hughes walked. The men who taught because they loved to teach, and the students who studied because they loved to learn. She saw it all, of course, through rose-colored glasses, and spent there the happiest of years."

There was Lillie: four young children and another on the way, a mother-in-law on her hands, a husband who was in the process of giving up a profitable business to tackle one that might never pay much more than a bare living—and "of course" she saw it all through rose-colored glasses. She *always* saw the world that way.

Perhaps because she couldn't cook at all, Lillie was also greatly impressed by the housewives she met in Providence.

From time to time, she'd march bravely into the kitchen, cookbook in hand, to prepare a special surprise. But invariably she'd emerge with a burnt or cut finger and some fudge that wouldn't harden or a bowl of hopelessly curdled junket.

"Don't apologize, Boss," Frank told her one morning when she decided she'd personally prepare his oatmeal. "Ever since my Sunday School days I've been wondering what a mess of pottage looked like."

So Lillie really meant it when she wrote: "The New England housewife! She is able to preside at woman's club or speak before school or association with poise and ease, and equally able to preside over the preserving kettle, while concocting such delectable doughnuts, apple pies, and queen puddings as are found nowhere else."

Several months after Lillie enrolled at Brown, Frank sent her thesis to the magazine *Industrial Engineering,* which started publishing it in installments. She was listed as L. M. Gilbreth, and there was no mention that she was a woman. Her "human" approach to scientific management attracted immediate attention, and when acquaintances of Frank would ask him if he were related to L. M. Gilbreth, he'd reply, "Only by marriage."

At about the same time, Frank and Lillie attended the first Conference on Scientific Management, held at Dartmouth College. Taylor's disciples and lieutenants were there en masse, too. At the final session, the chairman, Morris Llewellyn Cooke, scared the wits out of Lillie by departing from the prepared program and announcing: "We have been watching the quiet work of one individual who has been working along lines apparently absolutely different from those being followed by any other worker in scientific management—and I wonder if Lillian Gilbreth would like to say a few words about her work."

Lillie was unprepared, and the job wasn't made any easier

by the knowledge that much of the audience thought a woman shouldn't even be present, let alone asked to talk. Nervous as she was, she managed to outline briefly some ideas about how colleges could work with industry to improve management techniques.

Frank, who was a scheduled speaker, was so proud that when his turn came he grinned, shook his head, and said he was "speechless." But, Gilbreth fashion, he wasn't so speechless that he didn't eventually give his speech.

Yes, those *were* the "happiest of years." And if Lillie couldn't excel in the kitchen as she did in the Brown classrooms, the fault was partly Frank's.

"Don't waste your time on housework, Boss," he'd tell her. "Under our three-position plan of promotion, you're studying for *my* job."

Under this plan, which Frank had devised for his contracting business, the man immediately above you was training you for his job, while you were training the man below you for yours. Frank never said what job *he* was studying for, but it goes without saying that Lillie's training eventually stood her in good stead.

So Grandma supervised the kitchen, assisted by Annie Cunningham and Tom Grieves, the cook and handyman. There also were a splendid governess, a second maid, and a part-time laundress. Also, a hairdresser came in once a week to give Lillie and the girls shampoos.

After Bill was born, Tom Grieves was assigned as my none-too-gentle shampooer, and eventually Tom became the official shampooer for all the boys.

We practically worshipped Tom, and I'm sure that in many ways the affection was requited. But he was so afraid that Bill and I would grow up to be sissies—having three older sisters and a grandmother on the premises, as well as a mother—that he deemed it his bounden duty to teach us a proper vocabulary at a tender age.

He'd shampoo us with a stiff brush while we sat in a bathtub, and occasionally he would grab our noses, duck us, and swish us back and forth under water for rinsing.

"I ought to have a Goddam *brick,* for Christ sake, instead of this brush to get you little bastids clean," he'd mutter.

The servants were kept busy, because the house was usually full of guests as well as children. Frank was now well known on college campuses all over the country, and Lillie was becoming known, so our house was a gathering spot for professors, management people, and what today would be known as eggheads in general.

Among the visitors were also a number of athletes whose motions Frank had studied with movies. They included Francis Ouimet and Harry Varden, the golfers; Walter Camp, who picked the first All-American football team and originated the Daily Dozen exercises; and Christy Mathewson, the Giant pitcher.

Frank used to say he won a five-dollar bet from Ouimet by proving with the movies that he ducked his head nine-sixteenths of an inch on every shot.

Often the guests would stay for meals, and Martha liked to see people eat well. Her breakfasts, for instance, besides hot cereal and eggs, usually included johnnycakes and something like apple pie or strawberry shortcake. Lunch and supper would be full-course meals, and for snacks a pot of beans and a dozen sweet potatoes usually were kept hot at the back of the stove and oven, respectively.

Down in the basement near the big coal furnace, Martha had converted a whole room into a pantry filled with homemade preserves, jellies, pickles, ketchup, and wonderful sauces. And Mrs. Cunningham made fresh bread every day.

Whether or not there was company for a meal, Frank would put us children through our paces. He had his own day divided into time-segments of productive work, recreation, rest, and "unavoidable delay." Eating, dressing, and bathroom-occupancy were all unavoidable delay—and Frank thought this time should be used for mental development.

So we had phonographs in the boys' bathroom, the girls' bathroom, and the bedrooms, to play foreign language records; and we had two bookcases full of reference works in the dining room to settle arguments which might develop from discussions and games that Frank would direct.

Another of Frank's rules was that only matters of general interest could be discussed at meals. And since he had appointed himself sole arbiter of what *was* of general interest, he pretty well monopolized the conversation. A child who refused to accept the arbiter's decision, and sought to argue the matter, was apt to be beaned firmly by Frank's knuckles. Three beans at one meal meant automatic ejection from the dining room.

Arithmetic, naturally, was deemed of general interest. Dad had taught all of us some easy tricks of mental math. If the dinner guests were engineers, he'd often pit us against them —and without pencils and paper or their slide rules, they were dead.

"Forty-nine times forty-nine," Dad would bellow, stopwatch in hand for all the world like a Taylor disciple. And as our hands were raised practically simultaneously, he'd click the stopwatch and say, "Two seconds. Pretty good, kids. Tell them the answer."

And we'd say the answer was 2401, because we knew that when you are squaring, for instance, a number close to 50, all you have to say to yourself is, "How much more is 49 than 25? Twenty-four, right? And how much less is it than 50? One, right? Square the one and you get one. So the answer is 2401."

Another example: 47 times 47. Forty-seven is 22 more than 25, and three less than 50. Square the three and get nine. So the answer is 2209. And still another: 54 times 54. Fifty-four is 29 more than 25 and four more than 50. Square the four, and get 16, which gives you 2916.

It may sound complicated, but it isn't, when you get used to it. Anyway this and a series of other math tricks never ceased to amaze the visitors, and were always of general interest.

One psychologist who often visited us used to like to give word-association tests at meals. He couldn't believe his ears when Anne and my third oldest sister, Martha, shouted "factory" as the word they associated with "plant."

"I guess there may be tens of thousands of flowers in the world, running all the way from asters to zinnias," he told Lillie, "but your children think of factories. Are you sure that's wise?"

"If you had used the term 'botanical plants,'" Lillie said gently, "perhaps they would have answered anything from asters to zinnias."

One of Lillie's favorite games at meals was to dress up a proverb or popular saying in multisyllable rhetoric, and see who could figure it out. She made up some of these herself and obtained others from books. For instance, she'd say:

> Who counts ere fractured are the shells
> Of bipeds gallinaceous
> Is apt to find his calculations
> Utterly fallacious.

We were supposed to deduce that you shouldn't count chickens before they were hatched. Also:

> A futile superfluity
> Of culinary aid
> Destroys nutritious liquids
> Of osseous tissues made.

That, of course, referred to the saying about too many cooks. Frank also thought that a good vocabulary was important, and had a story about a former chorus girl who married an engineer acquaintance of his. She looked and acted like a lady, he said, but gave herself away with embarrassing malapropisms, one of which was using the word "costive" when she meant "expensive." When we asked what "costive" meant, he made us look it up. And when we did so, and found that it meant "constipated," and then laughed hilariously, Mother called him and us Eskimos, which was her word for anything off-color or racy.

As for Motion Study, that was of such *especial* general interest that discussions often moved from the dining room to the living room, after a meal. If there were guests, Frank would usually illustrate his points with micromotion studies.

"Here's the problem I'm working on right now," he would say. "No, I haven't been *hired* to do it—not yet. But anyway they let me take some pictures. Nowadays everything is soapflakes, right? So these boxes of soapflakes come down a conveyor belt. Women sit along the belt, take the boxes, and put them in large cartons. Let me show you a motion picture. All right, kids, get the projector and equipment."

Each of us had an assigned chore when this order was given. Film was extremely flammable in those days, so my job, as a toddler, was to bring in a bucket of sand. The youngest, Bill, eventually would understudy me as sandman, under the three-position plan of promotion, and I was understudying Martha, who set up the tripod for the hand-cranked projector. Anne and Ernestine got the projector itself and the screen.

After Frank threaded the projector and we put out the lights and pulled the shades, Anne started cranking, and pictures of women packing the soapflakes came on the screen.

"You see," Frank explained, "they used to pick up a box in each hand and put them into the carton. This is how they used to do it. Now the sequence coming up shows how I have them doing it. The cartons are raised so the women don't have to lean over. And they pick up two boxes in each hand. But there's the problem—watch now, and you can see it. One hand gets in the way of the other hand, as they put four boxes in the carton. How do we lick that?"

He turned off the projector, and he, Mother, and their friends discussed it.

Then my sister Martha, who wasn't much more than a toddler herself, pulled at Lillie's skirt and said that *she* had an idea. Lillie believed in listening patiently to her children, and told Mart that she had the floor.

"Give each woman two cartons to fill," said Mart. "Let her fill one with one hand and the other with the other hand, and the hands won't get in each other's way, I bet."

There was silence for about thirty seconds, while our parents and the other engineers thought it over. And Mart's answer was so obvious that everyone wondered why he hadn't thought of it first.

"By jingo," Frank exclaimed. "Well, by jingo! Say, Lillie, is that little red-headed girl with the freckles, who just said that, one of our kids?"

"Aw, you know I am, Daddy," Mart protested.

"A chip off the old block," he crowed. "You know, Boss, I believe we ought to *keep* that one!"

He fished in his vest pocket, where he sometimes carried a five-dollar gold piece, and found one there. He flipped it through the air to Martha. "There you are, Mart." Then he added, as he always did when tipping, "Go buy yourself a good cigar."

CHAPTER 11

Hipped on Motion Study

Shortly after Frank started work for the Butt Company, he took a month off so that he and Lillie could go to Europe together and attend a joint summer meeting in England of the A.S.M.E. and the British Institution of Mechanical Engineers.

Henry L. Gantt, who also played an important role in developing scientific management, crossed the ocean with them, and they became good friends. Gantt originally was a Taylor disciple, but then formed his own organization. However, he was familiar enough with the Taylor-Gilbreth feud to tease Frank about being "hipped on Motion Study" and to tease Lillie about being "hipped on the human element."

"Of course we're hipped," Frank replied. "And, Gantt, if you knew as much as we do about it, you'd be hipped too."

Gantt's reference to Lillie was the result of a letter L. M.

Gilbreth had written to one of the scientific magazines urging union leaders to "study, foster, and cultivate" scientific management. She added that otherwise "unscrupulous managers" would reap all the benefits, and working people would get none.

In London, Gantt and the Gilbreths visited the Japanese-British Exposition, where one of the exhibits featured the manufacture of shoe polish. One phase of the operation involved pasting labels on boxes of polish, and a Japanese girl who performed this on a piecerate basis was such a speed merchant that she invariably attracted crowds.

"There you are, Gilbreth," Gantt challenged Frank— "what could Motion Study do for her?"

Frank watched her for a while. He saw that, although she was dexterous and moved like lightning, she was reaching too far with one hand to get the boxes and too far with the other to get the labels. Meanwhile, Gantt had palmed his stopwatch and was timing her.

"She does twenty-four boxes in forty seconds," Gantt said.

Frank held a whispered conversation with Lillie, and then told Gantt, "I'll bet you a guinea she can do a box a second."

Gantt agreed, and Frank waited until the crowd had thinned. Then he stopped the girl, and asked permission to rearrange her materials. When she nodded, he shifted the boxes and the labels, and then took her little hands in his.

"Now," he said, "move this way, and *this* way, and when you finish the box, just flick it off the table onto the floor, like *this*."

She nodded again and tried it, quickly picking up speed as she became accustomed to the new motions. Gantt clicked his stopwatch. She was going at a speed of twenty-four boxes in twenty-six seconds. He timed her again: twenty-six boxes in twenty seconds.

Gantt handed Frank the equivalent of a guinea, twenty-one shillings, and Frank gave the Japanese girl a ten-shilling note. "Buy yourself a good cigar," he winked.

"And you see, Gantt," he gloated, "she isn't working any harder at her new rate than her old—in fact, not quite so hard, because her motions are shorter. And what I've been trying to get through your head and Taylor's is . . ."

"Hipped on Motion Study," sighed Gantt.

But Lillie still wasn't completely satisfied. "You only gave her ten shillings—and that's not half of twenty-one," she told Frank. "What's half of one shilling—sixpence?"

Frank nodded, found a sixpence in his pocket, and gave it to the tittering Japanese girl.

"Buy yourself another cigar—not quite as good," he said.

"Hipped," nodded Gantt. "You're both *hipped!*"

Luckily, Frank was well paid for his job at the Butt Company, because almost all the money he received for his contracting business went for cameras, a small motion picture studio, projectors, and laboratories for photography and Motion Study.

The general manager of the Butt Company, John G. Aldrich, was immediately impressed by the way Frank enlisted the cooperation and support of employes. Instead of slinking around with a stopwatch in his pocket, Frank called all the men together and told them in advance just what he proposed to do—and explained how they themselves would profit from increased production.

Frank's experiments with fatigue had also convinced him that two rest periods a day—the forerunner of the coffee break—increased production. And this innovation solidified the support of both the employes and the union leaders.

Aldrich, who was a progressive engineer himself, became

extremely interested in the micromotion studies Gilbreth was making at his own expense, and the manager cooperated in every way with these.

But two Taylor lieutenants, who had been personally assigned to the job by the "father of scientific management," were all but horrified that Gilbreth was deviating from the precise and well documented procedures that Taylor disciples were supposed to employ.

The two immediately reported to Taylor that Gilbreth was persisting in his "mysterious" activities with motion picture machines. Taylor protested sharply to Frank—but Frank went ahead with his experiments anyway, apparently figuring that this might be his only chance to obtain the necessary footage of film to prove the worth of his own methods.

The two Taylor lieutenants had been trained by Horace K. Hathaway, a full-fledged disciple. Hathaway wrote Taylor that he had had plenty of doubts about Gilbreth from the beginning, and that he was now convinced that Frank "had no business whatsoever to undertake the systemizing of a large company, without having any experience in that field."

Taylor also apparently had become convinced of that. Since Frank wouldn't listen to him, Taylor wrote Aldrich himself that Gilbreth's "photographic scheme" might cause workmen to strike.

Aldrich knew from personal observation that the micromotion studies weren't causing labor troubles, so he allowed Frank to proceed.

As the films were developed, Frank always showed them to the employes, so they'd understand what he was trying to accomplish. Standing up front at the screen with a pointer in his hand, he'd rely on the sort of over-hearty humor that came naturally to him, and went over so well.

"This handsome, curly-haired fellow walking on screen

now," he'd say, while the men whooped and the bald-headed object of the whoops grinned self-consciously, "is Bill Fredericks. Now look. Right here Bill's going to brush the hair out of his eyes."

There'd be another whoop as Bill, on screen, rubbed his bald head. In the background, of course, were the four-inch squares and the Gilbreth clock.

"Now we've always believed that the man with the best motions on any job is the laziest scoundrel around. Why? Because he's too lazy to *waste* motions. Well, naturally, when we looked for the laziest galoot running a lathe here at the Butt Company, everyone referred us right away to Bill."

More whoops!

"No, seriously, Bill isn't lazy—although sometimes it's true that the laziest man has the best motions. Bill is one of the hardest-working lathe operators in Providence. I've been to a lot of factories, and I never saw a man who could get any more out of a lathe than Bill. We picked him so we could see *why* he's such a good operator, and to see if we could change the lathe around any to make him an even *better* operator."

So Aldrich could certainly vouch for the fact that this sort of approach was less apt to cause trouble than that of the whispering time-study sleuths and their hidden watches.

Aside from the micromotion studies, the most important management tool introduced by Gilbreth at the Butt Company was the process or flow chart, which he and Lillie devised.

Process charts are still used in practically every industry today, and they have been changed very little if at all. The charts show graphically, among other things, the arrival of materials at a factory and each step in their treatment as they move from machine to machine and emerge as the final product. Any bottlenecks or backtrackings in the production flow become immediately apparent.

Another of the Gilbreths' ideas, the Home Reading Box, was also installed. This was simply a large, topless box, in which all employes were urged to deposit their old magazines, and to help themselves to any issues they hadn't read. Frank thought the Reading Box was good for employe relations, and had some educational and recreational advantages.

There was certainly nothing earth-shaking or policy-setting about collecting and distributing old magazines, but since the Reading Box wasn't included in Dr. Taylor's system it was ridiculed and criticized unmercifully. For instance, Leon Alford, a Taylor supporter, called it a "trash basket." He also wrote in the *American Machinist,* which he edited, that "Gilbreth's Box" attracted mostly magazines of the "lighter variety."

Although some people might have considered this more of a virtue than a sin, Frank rose swiftly to the bait. He wrote Alford that, after exhaustive research, he had reached the inevitable conclusion that the most un-light periodical on the market—both from the standpoint of scientific illumination and downright dreariness—was Alford's selfsame *American Machinist.* "We have collected so many of them [in the Home Reading Box] they are a drug on the market," Frank added. "Lighter variety indeed! Who has been jollying you?"

When Frank finally completed his job at the Butt Company, General Manager Aldrich congratulated him and said he'd done a splendid service both to the company and to management in general. But the Taylor group kept circulating reports that Gilbreth had overcharged and bungled.

As these reports kept reaching Aldrich, he became more and more annoyed. Finally he decided to set the record straight, and chose the next annual meeting of the A.S.M.E.

as his sounding board, so that there couldn't be any misunderstanding about his position.

At that meeting, Aldrich said that Gilbreth *hadn't* overcharged or bungled, and that micromotion was the "least expensive as well as the only accurate method of recording motion and time study data." He also cited one particular operation at his plant which Gilbreth had shortened from thirty-seven and a half to eight and a half minutes.

This endorsement apparently took Taylor by surprise, because he had been informed otherwise by some of his disciples. But Disciple Hathaway promptly wrote Taylor that if, indeed, the job at the Butt Company had been successful, "practically all the credit is due Shipley." Albert R. Shipley was one of the two Taylor lieutenants assigned to the project.

Frank's next job was with Hermann, Aukam Company, handkerchief manufacturers, and this time the Taylor organization actually succeeded in getting him fired.

With the help of micromotion studies, Frank reduced the number of motions required to fold handkerchiefs from one hundred and fifty to sixteen. But he had a violent disagreement with one of the owners, M. C. Hermann, about the pay scale for the increased production. Frank asserted bluntly that the profits resulting from his studies were "all hogged by the owner," and that he simply wouldn't stand for that.

Both Gilbreths were already on record—Lillie in *The Psychology of Management* and Frank in the *Primer of Scientific Management*—as insisting that workers be given their share of any profits accruing from the Gilbreth System. To cut the workers out of such profits, Frank declared, was "cutting the throat of the goose that laid the golden eggs."

Frank tried to explain to Hermann the Gilbreths' beliefs

about "Happiness Minutes." He pointed out that "if every member of the organization, including the manager and the stockholders, is getting more 'Happiness Minutes,' you surely are working along the right line."

But apparently Mr. Hermann was unimpressed, because he appealed to Taylor, saying that Frank's fees were exorbitant. The upshot was that Frank's contract was canceled, and Taylor sent Hathaway to take over in Frank's stead.

When Hathaway arrived at the handkerchief factory, he threw up his hands in mock disbelief, and said that between Gilbreth and micromotion study the whole operation had been hopelessly demoralized. As for Frank himself, Hathaway declared he was "either raving crazy or a fakir."

The result was that Frank couldn't immediately find another client, although he was saddled with his heavy household and laboratory expenses.

Not content with this, Dr. Taylor also sought to discredit Frank in the academic world. The Gilbreths had started the first of four popular, tuition-free, and well attended summer schools on the psychology of managment, for college teachers, at our house in Providence. In addition, many colleges had expressed interest in that subject and in micromotion study. Taylor wrote Professor Lionel S. Marks of Harvard not to "lay too great stress" on the work being done by Gilbreth, because Frank was solely interested in money and was "likely to do great harm to our cause."

Nevertheless, the academic world seemed to have more of a rapport with the Gilbreths, who kept seeking new ideas, than with Taylor, who had virtually closed the door to change once his own system was devised.

When Frank found that Taylor had all but blacklisted him with American industries, he signed contracts with German General Electric and Zeiss, despite complaints in the German press that he intended to "Americanize" European industry. On every trip to Europe, Frank also visited hospitals and took motion pictures—at his own expense—of the best surgeons at work.

Some of Taylor's disciples urged Dr. Taylor to write friends in Europe and get Gilbreth practically blacklisted over there, too. Disciples Hathaway and Carl Barth said Taylor should "expose" Gilbreth in Europe as a "fakir" and "fraud." But Taylor had become ill, and for some reason decided he wouldn't carry the feud any further. "I agree with you that he might discredit the whole movement in Germany," he wrote Barth, "and yet it seems hard to write and point out his incompetence."

Taylor died in 1915. Up to that time, Frank had mostly been turning the other cheek, because of his deep respect for the "father of scientific management." He had no such respect, though, for some of the disciples—and they soon found that their whipping boy was now swinging a whip of his own.

Some of the disciples, Frank said in his speeches, were for Time Study and against Motion Study because they were "interested in the profits from the sale of stopwatches, time study devices, or books describing stopwatch time study methods."

When Frank started to fight back at his tormentors, some of them became eager for a truce.

"Is it wise, even from the sordid viewpoint of good business policy, to damn Taylor and all his works up hill and down before large audiences?" Disciple Thompson wrote Frank. "You and we are working for the same end . . . ."

That was the first time anyone in the Taylor group had conceded that the Gilbreth System was any more than fak-

ery, and Frank wrote Thompson that his "smooth and tact-
ful" words had been well received.

But years later, as Lillie was to discover when Frank in
turn died, the Gilbreth-Taylor feud was a long way from
being ended.

CHAPTER 12

Expectant Doctor

Lillie received her Ph.D. from Brown in the spring of 1914, but there was some doubt, right up to the last day, whether she would be marching in the graduation processional or having another baby.

However, the baby waited and Lillie marched—much to the disapproval of Grandma, who thought expectant mothers should stay in seclusion.

"I must admit, though," the outspoken Martha said, "that if Lillie feels she *has* to appear in public, a graduation gown is practically designed for the occasion. It will hide"—she surveyed Lillie's figure critically—"well, almost hide, her condition."

So Lillie marched, Frank burst with pride, and Grandma played a game of musical chairs with our cribs and beds, so that we all moved up to a larger size—and the smallest crib was vacated and made ready for the new arrival.

Lillie gave birth to her namesake three days after she became a doctor.

As the family grew, Frank decided that the One Best Way to keep all of us on our toes was to install the Gilbreth System in the home. So he established a Home Reading Box, gave us all file numbers, and drew up process and weight charts for us.

Our guests as well as the family itself were encouraged to use the Reading Box, which often bulged with a dozen or so new and identical issues of a technical magazine which happened to contain an article by Frank himself.

"Look at them!" Frank would sometimes complain to Lillie, pointing at the untouched issues in the Reading Box. "I'll swear even Alford's *American Machinist* moves faster than those. You'd think that even if nobody around here wants to *read* my article, at least someone would do me the courtesy of making them look dog-eared."

The purpose of the file numbers was so Frank's secretaries would know where—among his office records—to file each child's birth certificate, vaccination certificate, Sunday School diploma, school report cards, etc. Frank also used the numbers so that he could easily route memoranda to the children concerned, and so that he and Lillie wouldn't be confused with their namesakes on the routing slips.

Dad himself was file number seven, since he was born on the seventh day of the seventh month. Lillie was seven-L, Anne was eight, Ern nine, Mart ten, and so forth.

Our process and weight charts were thumbtacked to the walls of the boys' and girls' bathrooms, and were supposed to improve our efficiency, and to let our parents know where we were and whether we were in good health.

Frank maintained that a regimented schedule was needed,

especially in the mornings when there was apt to be lolling in the bathtubs.

He had cut his own bathroom time considerably by making Motion Studies of his bathing and shaving. He now lathered his face with two brushes, one in each hand. Sometimes, fully clothed, he'd also climb into an imaginary bathtub in the parlor and demonstrate how to bathe.

With a certain amount of seal-like bellowing, as if he were blowing droplets from his lips, he'd grasp an imaginary bar of soap and tell us:

"I put the soap in my right hand, like this, and then I start on the left side of my neck. Now bring the soap down the top of your left arm, and up the bottom of your left arm. Then down your left side . . ."

"But sometimes," I once told him, "it's fun to lie around in the tub without thinking of any old One Best Ways."

"Sure it is, Frank-o," he agreed. "But not with four or five people waiting. Any time you want to loll, just check the charts for a time when no one's waiting."

Lillie was the kind of mother who always knew, sometimes seemingly by instinct, where each child was at any given time, so the process charts may not have been much help to her as a child-locator. Frank and Martha, however, found them invaluable. If they wanted to know what each member of the brood was doing at, for instance, 4:42 on a Wednesday afternoon, they simply located the 4:42 time level and observed that Anne was taking a violin lesson, Ern was at dancing school, Martha at basketball practice, etc.

My own process chart for any given Wednesday morning might show:

> 7:00—Rise and shine. Mart will call you.
> 7:01—Your turn in bathroom.

7:02—Play German records while brushing teeth, bathing, and other unavoidable delay.
7:03—Did you remember to wash your ears?
7:07—Weigh self and post on weight chart.
7:08—Comb hair, wash ring out of tub, start bath for Bill, wind Graphophone.
7:10—Wake Bill.
7:11—Play French records in bedroom while dressing.
7:16—Shine shoes.
7:18—Make bed.
7:21—Straighten room.
7:31—Eat breakfast.
And so forth.

This may sound about as gay and informal as a concentration camp, but it really seemed more like a game at the time. And, after all, children are imitative, and this was the sort of thing that our parents and their friends discussed all day long.

It was a game, too, to see if you could beat the schedule of your process chart so that you'd have ten or twelve minutes of rest and relaxation between "straighten room" and "eat breakfast." This gave you an opportunity to read *Happy Hooligan, Krazy Kat,* and the other funnies, while playing popular records on the downstairs phonograph—provided Dad hadn't taken it apart or broken the spring again. He kept tinkering with a little motor he had rigged to replace the hand crank, but the motor wouldn't always shut off when it was supposed to, and thus kept snapping the spring.

The only member of the household who wasn't impressed by the process charts was Tom Grieves.

" 'Wash ring out of tub, start bath for Bill,' " he'd quote

my process chart, while scrubbing the bathtub himself with a rag and a cake of Sapolio. "Nobody but me never washed a Goddam tub around here in their whole lives, for Christ sake. And then, 'Shine shoes and make bed.' What you little bastids do is shine the floor and mess the bed and . . ."

Then, hearing Mother approach, he'd switch quickly into the goody-good vocabulary he reserved for her, Mrs. Cunningham, and in fact most females.

". . . goodness me, Frankie-boy," Tom would continue, "this Sapolio is really a peachy soap. Gracious, it makes the whole house look like Spotless Town, for mercy sake . . ."

And then as Mother disappeared again:

". . . Yeah, the only rings that get washed around here are by me, Goddammit. You little bastids can fool your Mother and you can fool your Father, but you can't fool me. You know what Motion Study is, Frankie-boy? You study how to get somebody else to make all your motions for you, for Christ sake."

Two weeks after Lillie received her doctor's degree, Archduke Ferdinand was assassinated in Sarajevo, and Europe was at war. As the casualties mounted, Frank and Lillie realized that for a generation to come there would be hundreds of thousands of terribly unhappy amputees throughout the Old World. And since the Gilbreths were both "hipped on Motion Study," they began to wonder whether they couldn't employ their new techniques to make more bearable the lives of these "crippled soldiers," as the men were then called.

Commenting recently on the Gilbreths' initial efforts to help the amputees of World War I, Dr. Howard A. Rusk, chairman of the Department of Rehabilitation Medicine, New York University School of Medicine, said that these efforts actually "laid the basis for modern rehabilitation services for the physically handicapped."

Just as he had earlier told employers that they should reduce fatigue and increase the pay of their workers, Frank now took it upon himself to tell his own colleagues what he deemed to be their responsibilities in dealing with the handicapped. Speaking to the American Association for the Advancement of Science in December 1915, he said that it was not only their duty but their "privilege" to show "cripples" how they could become productive.

He said that when a crippled soldier was discharged, the "securing of his usefulness, efficiency, and *happiness* becomes a problem for the engineer, the Motion Study expert, and for the industries."

Frank added that even if the warring countries could eventually afford to pension their cripples, that wouldn't be enough.

"The last thing in the world the sufferer wants is . . . idleness," he said. "The great horror of the majority of injured soldiers is that of becoming non-productive members of the community, allowed to exist on sufferance."

So at our house in Providence, the Motion Study movies now began to feature amputees. Often the films were terribly depressing—but not as depressing as some later ones, made of the blind and of people in mental institutions.

A man without any arms would be pictured on the improvised screen in our parlor. The wall behind him, as always, was marked off in four-inch squares, and the Gilbreth clock was in the background.

"The first thing a man wants to do when he becomes a cripple," Frank would tell us and his friends, "is to take care of himself. We can think about getting him a job later. But first we've got to get him in and out of his pants. So that was the first thing we taught Freddy Appleseed here—that's really his name, too. Watch him."

Freddy walked over to a rack with two waist-high hooks on it, and the hooks fitted into loops which had been sewed at the top of his trousers. Built into the rack was a short step-ladder. As Freddy ascended the ladder, he emerged from his trousers like a snake shedding its skin. The trousers were left dangling on the hooks, presumably for use the next morning, and Freddy descended the ladder, looking rather sheepish in a pair of long-johns.

"The top of the pants is made of elastic," Frank explained. "He doesn't have any buttons, belt, or suspenders to worry about. Don't be afraid, ladies, I'm not going to show you how he takes off his underwear, but we've taught him that, too."

"Eskimo!" said Lillie.

"Incidentally," Frank continued, as if he hadn't heard her, "there's a good-looking baby-doll at the hospital who lost the tip of her little finger in a cigar-cutter. She keeps after me to make a dress rack for her, and take pictures . . ."

"Eskimo!" Lillie repeated sternly. But she couldn't help smiling, just the same, and she knew that Frank was anything but callous, and was laying on his heavy-handed humor because he didn't want the movies to put us or his guests in a depressed mood.

At the end of the film, with Freddie looking relieved to be wearing his pants again, we put the lights back on.

Then Frank asked: "All right, he can dress and undress himself, but what kind of a job can he do? Sing them out, and I'll write them down."

"An usher in a theater."

"How would he hand out programs?"

"He could carry an open pouch around his neck, and you could help yourself."

"An overseer on a construction job."

"How would he write his reports?"

"Dictaphone."

"How would he turn it off and on?"

"Build him a foot pedal."

"If he's smart enough to dictate, he could be an office manager, too."

"Could he run a drill press if we rigged pedals instead of handles?"

"Give him Tom's job, for Christ's sake," one young boy whose name I'd better not mention observed. "All he does is stand around and complain anyway, the old bastid."

"Why, aren't you *ashamed* of yourself!" Lillie almost shouted, incredulously. "Where in the *world* could you *possibly* have learned language like that! I know you'll want to apologize, dear, to everyone here. And besides that, it isn't fair to Tom, who works so hard and *never* complains."

"Goodness gracious, no," said Frank, who had managed to smother a guffaw in his handkerchief. "Land sakes and mercy me. Tom's a peachy man."

After Dr. Taylor's death, Frank soon lined up all the American clients he could handle. Eastman Kodak, Cluett Peabody, Lever Brothers, U. S. Rubber, and Pierce Arrow were among his employers. And if he and Lillie were spending tens of thousands of dollars on their studies of the handicapped, at least they were being well paid by their industrial clients. Frank readily admitted that he was one of the most highly paid consultants in the world, and even more readily admitted that no one deserved it more. "Besides, they're getting two of us for the price of one," he told Lillie. "Anyway, you keep saying that workers should share in the benefits of scientific management. Well, aren't we workers? So aren't we entitled to some Happiness Minutes of our own?"

He developed the fastest typists in the world for the Remington Company, and they won prizes against all comers in contests at New York and Chicago.

In the process, all the Gilbreth children had to study touch-typing at home—partly for their own benefit and partly because Frank had two theories he wanted to try. One was that touch-typing could be taught by putting blank caps, in which different designs of pinholes had been punched, over the keys. He hoped that the typist's fingers would thus seek out the right keys, in somewhat the same way that a blind person reads Braille. The other theory involved putting caps of different colors on the keys—and then painting the fingers that were to use those keys with corresponding colors. The Gilbreth children may have been the first to show up at school with multi-tinted fingernails.

He had some success with both theories, but wasn't completely satisfied with either.

To study the motions of speed typists, Frank and Lillie used a new device which they invented and called a chrono-cyclegraph. This consisted of a small flashing light, attached to a hand, finger, or moving part of a machine being studied. Then a time-exposure picture was taken of a complete motion or "cycle." The finished photographic print showed, in the form of a dotted white line on a black background, the exact path of the motion in two dimensions. By taking the photographs stereoscopically, the motions were shown in three dimensions. The lights flashed a specific number of times a second, and by counting the number of dots on the photograph—and measuring the distance between them—it was possible to determine not only time and speed, but also acceleration and retardation.

By the right combination of volts and amperes, and by experimenting with the thickness of the filaments in the tiny lightbulbs, Frank made the lights come on almost instantaneously and go out slowly. This put an arrow and a comet-like tail on each dot in the photographed motion line, and thus he was able to indicate direction as well as the other factors.

Just before the United States entered World War I, Frank and Lillie isolated the components in a motion cycle, and named them therbligs. Micromotion, the chronocyclegraph, and the therbligs were the heart of the Gilbreth System.

Originally, they thought there were sixteen components in a motion cycle—Search, Find, Select, Grasp, Position, Assemble, Use, Disassemble, Inspect, Transport Loaded, Preposition for Next Operation, Release Load, Transport Empty, Wait (unavoidable delay), Wait (avoidable delay), and Rest (necessary for overcoming fatigue). A few years later they added one more component: Plan.

The therbligs came into almost universal use among management men seeking specific areas, within a motion cycle, in which to speed production. Frank himself used the therblig technique to reduce the operating time of surgeons.

In the days before Motion Study, a surgeon might have started a motion cycle by switching his eyes from the incision in the patient to a nearby table where his instruments were spread out. That's therblig No. 1: Search.

His eyes would pick out, from the various instruments, the specific one he needed. That's No. 2: Find.

He would reach over with his hand and touch the instrument he needed. No. 3: Select.

Then he would actually pick up the instrument. No. 4: Grasp. Etc.

Seeking to eliminate as many components as possible in the motion cycle, Frank saw quite quickly that he could eliminate the first three—Search, Find, and Select—by having the doctor put out his hand, palm-up, and having a nurse place the instrument in his hand. And if all of that seems elementary today, the fact is that the Gilbreths' techniques reduced some operating times by as much as two-thirds, thus minimizing deaths which often resulted from such things as complications due to prolonged anesthesia.

A few years after the therbligs became a part of the Gilbreth System, someone noticed that "therblig" was "Gilbreth" spelled backward, with a slight variation. Frank was then accused of being a publicity hound, by trying to get his name into the language, even if spelled backward.

Frank wouldn't have denied being a whole pack of publicity hounds, in full cry, for anything to do with Motion Study. But the fact is that he obtained the idea for the word "therblig" from a newspaper hoax which had occurred in New York.

It seems that the Associated Press and the United Press both suspected the International News Service of stealing their news dispatches. So the AP and the UP got together and created an imaginary ship named *Nelots*.

Graphic dispatches from a faraway ocean, carried separately by AP and UP, alleged that *Nelots* was ablaze and sinking. These stories were rewritten even more graphically by INS. After two or three days of this, AP and UP reported that *Nelots* had foundered in a final hiss of steam. INS promptly had the vessel going to Davy Jones' Locker in a holocaust of fire, while the captain's pet monkey perched on his shoulder and the cabin boy played "Nearer My God to Thee" on a borrowed mouth organ—or at any rate something pretty close to that.

Then the AP and the UP disclosed the humiliating truth —*Nelots* was "stolen" spelled backward; there never had been such a vessel; and all the graphic details in the INS dispatches were manufactured by an imaginative rewrite man.

So Frank thought he'd bait a similar trap for some of Taylor's disciples who, he was convinced, were stealing all his ideas.

He imagined, with a good deal of satisfaction, a confrontation which would take place when they claimed origination of his therbligs. Preferably, the confrontation would take place on an auditorium platform before a full house.

Frank would point an accusing finger at the culprit and say triumphantly: "So you invented the therbligs, eh? Well, let me show you something." Then he'd walk over to an imaginary blackboard and reverse the order of the letters, to the confounding of the culprit and deafening applause from the audience.

No wonder he was disappointed that someone had discovered his trap before it was sprung.

CHAPTER 13

The Major and His Pants

Fred was born shortly before the United States entered World War I, and Dan was on the way. Even so, Frank tried to get into the Army so that he could start the War Department on a program to rehabilitate "crippled soldiers."

In Washington, he had a long talk with the surgeon general, and showed him some of the films of Freddy Appleseed and others. But ostensibly because of his seven children—and perhaps also because he now weighed 230 pounds—the Army turned him down. The surgeon general asked him to volunteer again, though, if and when our country actually entered the war.

So when war was declared, Frank sent a telegram to President Wilson saying, "Arriving Washington 7:03 train. If you don't know how to use me, I'll tell you how."

Someone met him at the station, and within an hour or so he was sworn in as a major. When he got home again about a month later, he had lost at least ten pounds and had grown a toothbrush mustache, which still didn't succeed in making him look very military. The ten pounds didn't make it much easier, either, for him to lean over and wrap his leggings.

Around the house, we'd snap to attention and give him a stiff salute when he came into the room. And although he was in the Army for only a few months, he liked to be called "Major" for the rest of his life.

Back in Washington, he helped institute the Army's initial program of training films. The first of these showed rookies how to clean and assemble Lewis and Browning machine guns. Then he was transferred to Fort Sill, Oklahoma, where he continued making films. But he missed Lillie's assistance so much that he started sending some of his Army work to Providence, for her to handle.

Far from complaining that besides being pregnant she had her hands full at home trying to keep the business going and taking care of the seven children, Lillie wrote him: "It was almost the proudest moment of my life to be included in the Army work . . . . You are so wonderful to let me in on it, as you always do."

Frank wrote back enthusiastically: "I've got the best job in the Army . . . . What could be more interesting than a Lewis gun?"

But Frank then became deathly sick—first with rheumatism, then uremic poisoning, and finally pneumonia. Lillie got the bad news from Frank's assistant, Captain O. O. Ellis, who wired her despite Frank's orders to the contrary. It took her four days to reach the Army's makeshift hospital at Fort Sill. When she arrived, Frank was in a coma and the doctors didn't think he'd live. Lillie simply couldn't believe that, in the matter of just a few days, he could have gone from buoyant health to death's door.

The hospital was poorly equipped and packed with patients, many extremely ill and dying. Since there weren't any private rooms, Frank was in a bed in a long ward. In the intervals when he came out of his coma, he was delirious and had hallucinations.

In what may have been the first real act of aggressiveness in her life, Lillie took charge of the patient.

"Get him into a private room!" she ordered the hospital's commanding officer.

"I'm sorry, Mrs. Gilbreth, but we don't have any private rooms."

"Then get me a cot, and put it alongside of his bed," she snapped. "I'm moving into the ward."

"But you can't do that! This is the Army—and it's a *men's* ward. You can visit him, but . . ."

"I said," Lillie interrupted him, *"I'm moving into the ward.* If I have to sleep on the floor, I will. But *I'm moving in."*

The commanding officer surrendered, and told an orderly to get a cot, and to suspend some sheets from the ceiling, so as to give Major Gilbreth and his wife something resembling a private room.

Lillie soon found that the facilities were primitive, and that Frank had been the world's worst patient, and had alienated the entire staff before he became too sick to complain. He had said the kitchen was so dirty he wouldn't eat the food—so they had to send out to get special meals for him. They assigned him a private nurse, and he fired her. He said the laundry didn't get the sheets clean.

To make matters worse, Frank had infuriated much of the medical profession by asserting in a speech less than a year before that conditions in hospitals were "worse than in the average factory" and that "some hospitals are so bad they should be closed immediately." The speech had been delivered at a meeting of the American Medical Association, and was played up in the newspapers and the *Literary Digest.*

Of course the doctors at Fort Sill were doing their best for Frank, regardless of whatever pique they may have had. But they weren't doing well enough to suit Lillie.

"I want to hire two private nurses," she told the commanding officer of the hospital. "Where do I get them?"

"It's not as easy as that—they're awfully hard to find."

"I don't give a"—she hesitated because she had honestly never used language so strong before—"toot!" she exploded. "Not one single"—she decided to go the whole hog—"*darn* toot!" Tears had started to flow, but her voice didn't choke. She stamped her foot. "I don't care how hard they are to find. I want two private nurses, and I want them now."

"Yes ma'am," the commander said meekly.

"And what do I do if he has a crisis before the nurses come?"

"Adrenalin."

"How?"

He showed her.

"Get me some, please."

"Yes, ma'am."

Lillie lay down on the cot next to Frank, separated from the ward by the sheets, and held his hand. When he was delirious, she took notes of everything he said—because she knew he'd be interested if he recovered. In the past, Frank had taken moving pictures of patients in delirium and even during epileptic seizures, hoping that somehow they might add to medical knowledge.

An orderly brought the adrenalin, and within an hour the crisis came and she had to use it.

Eight years later, Lillie wrote in *The Quest:* "No words

can ever describe what happened there in that remote Army camp, in that poorly equipped hospital . . . . But they were fortunate to obtain two nurses who stood for all that is the finest in that splendid profession. One refused to give up even though she suffered cruelly from fallen arches. The other regarded the tired wife as well as the frightfully ill husband as a patient, and devoted herself unstintingly. Dear little mother of two boys, now in the Far West, nothing will ever make your help and kindness seem less precious."

It is typical that Lillie would have kept up with the nurse, even years later. She kept up with hundreds of people who had been nice to her at one time or another—sending little presents to their children and visiting or telephoning them when she passed through their towns.

Meanwhile, Martha was holding the fort in Providence. Luckily for her, the process charts kept the household running smoothly. And Tom Grieves, who had been a corporal in the Army during the Spanish-American War and was much impressed with Frank's rank of major, helped keep the children in line. We were simply wild about Tom, who could show you a hundred magic tricks, if you were good; and who, despite weighing only about a hundred and thirty pounds, said he could lick any man in Providence, and often on Saturday night tried to prove it, too.

Just the same, Martha had her hands full. She wrote a friend: "They are a fine lot of kids and I would like to live to see what path each will choose. They were all in bed with grippe for a while, but in due time got back to school. They were no sooner started again than six came down with measles . . . . I can't stop to tell you about myself. But I am perfectly well and, if I had to, could do as much as ever."

Frank suffered heart damage during his siege. His doctors told Lillie that he would always be bedridden—but she didn't believe it. For one thing, he hated that Fort Sill hospital so much that Lillie was sure, somehow, he'd walk out of it.

Within a few days, Lillie had won the support and sympathy of the doctors and the commanding officer. The latter stopped all planes from flying over the hospital and halted the Sunday afternoon band concert, because the noise seemed to disturb Lillie's patient.

When Frank became fully conscious again, he was as bad a patient as ever. Lillie had to buy set after set of new sheets, because he still didn't trust the laundry. He didn't trust the drinking water, either, so she had to bring him bottled water—and specially prepared meals.

"Boss," he kept telling her, "I've got to get out of here."

"Then rest and get better. You can do it."

"I'd give a million dollars just to be able to put on a pair of pants, and get out of this blasted nightgown."

"You'll do it sooner than you think—if you don't get yourself all excited. Rest and get better."

"I know now how Freddy Appleseed and some of those other handicapped people feel. Do you realize I'm handicapped myself?"

"You won't be for long."

"What I'd give for a pair of pants!"

Lillie got a pair of his trousers and hung them next to his bed, where he could touch them. The sheets suspended from the ceiling had been taken down, so everyone in the ward knew all about the major and his pants. Some of the men said he was "cuckoo."

The day finally came when he sat up, swung his legs over the side of the bed, reached for the trousers, and slid them on. He was still wearing them when Lillie, who had moved from the hospital to Frank's former quarters, came in with his lunch. That afternoon, the doctor brought him a pair of crutches, and Frank stood triumphantly on them for a couple of minutes, at the side of his bed, still in his pants.

The following day, Frank asked the doctor for the hundredth time when he could leave the hospital.

"I'll take the full responsibility if anything goes wrong," Frank promised. "Just cover me with a blanket, put me on the train, and when we get to Washington lift up the blanket and see what you have."

"I won't let you go until you're stronger. That's final."

"Well, when will that be?" Frank demanded.

"Damn it all, Major, how do I know?" snapped the doctor. "Let's just say you'll be strong enough when you can walk on crutches to the end of the ward and back. Believe me, we're just as anxious to get rid of you as you are to leave."

"Oh, no you're not!" said Frank. "Lillie, get my pants."

She got them, and helped him up. Frank wiggled painfully into the pants, and swung himself off the bed. Lillie handed him his crutches. He hobbled on them to the foot of his bed, and started painfully down the long corridor toward the end of the ward.

The cuckoo major, wearing his pants, was walking on crutches. The whole ward was silent, watching him. He was smiling confidently at the start, but after the first ten feet the smile was gone, and after the next ten feet, when he stopped for the first time to rest, he was grimacing in pain.

Lillie wrote in *The Quest*: "He walked to the end of the ward and back again, suffering untold agony, almost too weak to make a step, amid an odd silence, down the row of beds and back again, while the astonished doctor gasped, the little nurse fluttered after him, and the anxious but proud wife felt that the Frank she knew was coming back again."

Lillie packed Frank's things. Three orderlies carried and wheeled him to the train, and he and Lillie began the seemingly endless trip across the continent to Washington.

"Just as sunlight is brightest after a storm," Lillie wrote, "so is recovery most joyous after a dreadful illness."

When they arrived in Washington, Frank entered Walter Reed hospital, where he spent a few more weeks. And then the Army discharged him and sent him home—just in time for Lillie to have her baby.

Frank went back to work, but had to use crutches.

"I used to think, 'There but for the grace of God go I,' " he'd complain to Lillie when they were looking at films of the handicapped. "Now I can shorten it to just plain, 'There go I.' "

"But the big difference, dear," she soothed him, "is that you're getting better—and those poor souls never will. But they've learned not to feel sorry for themselves."

"The hell of being married to psychologists," Frank muttered, "is that they know how to tell you to stop feeling so blasted sorry for yourself, without telling you to stop feeling so blasted sorry for yourself."

"Yes, dear," Lillie conceded. "And think how much better it is to be hobbling around on crutches than to be in the Fort Sill hospital."

"God knows," Frank said devoutly, *"anything* is better than being in the Fort Sill Hospital. I'd rather be a basket case on the outside than be in that hell-hole with only a hangnail."

"Exactly," nodded Lillie. "So you see how lucky you are?"

"I'm just a lucky duck," said Frank, still a mite bitterly despite expert psychological treatment. "Sure, I'm so stiff I can hardly move, my joints are swollen, and a fat man—well, anyway, pleasingly plump—and crutches don't mix. But I'm a lucky duck."

"And so am I," smiled Lillie, "to have such a brave and cheerful husband who . . ."

"A lucky duck," repeated Frank, with a little less sarcasm.

"Next time, Boss, I'll have the baby and *you* join the Army and go to Fort Sill. I know one thing: I never want to be in a hospital again."

"I don't suppose anybody really looks forward to it, dear," the psychologist said mildly.

Frank remained on crutches for three or four months and had to use a cane for three or four more. The doctors told him and Lillie that the heart damage was permanent, and said he was on borrowed time. They urged him to take things easy—but that was something Frank simply couldn't do.

"Some people waste the best part of their lives trying to keep from dying," he told Lillie. "I don't have *time* for that."

In the postwar industrial expansion, hundreds of companies were looking for experienced management consultants, and for the first time the Gilbreths were able to pick and choose their clients. They also devoted more and more time to rehabilitation of the handicapped and to fostering safety in industry.

Since most of the new clients were in the New York area, and since the Providence house had become too small for the growing family, Frank called a meeting of the Family Council to discuss the wisdom of moving. The Council— composed of all hands and the cook, if you could give Martha that latter rating—made all major decisions, or at any rate it *thought* it did.

After considerable discussion, the Council authorized Dad to look for a house within easy commuting distance of New York, in a town where the schools were good.

Although he still maintained his amateur status, Dad wasn't a bad psychologist himself. So he managed to get carte blanche from the Council as a town-selector when actually he had already made a down-payment on a vast house in Montclair, New Jersey, where Gantt and a number of his other friends and colleagues lived.

All of the family but Grandma, who said that if necessary she'd rather crawl on her hands and knees, drove from Providence to Montclair in our gray Pierce Arrow touring car. Grandma, Tom Grieves, and Mrs. Cunningham all arrived separately by train.

Dad had named the Pierce Arrow "Foolish Carriage," because he said it was foolish for a man with a family as large as his to think he could afford such a fancy carriage. Mother, who was expecting another baby, sometimes must have thought that "Miss" would be a better first name than "Foolish," because Dad was both the world's worst and the world's most adventurous driver.

The car was equipped with a compact, homemade ice chest for baby bottles, and also with a specially tapered board which joined the folding swivel-seats in the back. The ice chest sat up front on the floor, near Mother's feet, and both it and the board provided extra seats for children.

Before we started on trips, we usually had speed drills to see whether we still had all our moxie when it came to putting up the isinglass side-curtains or changing a tire. We'd all be in the car, parked out front, and Dad would say, "All right, kids. Let's go with the curtains!" Then he'd press a stopwatch as we'd bail out, remove the front and back seats under which the curtains were stored, unfold the curtains themselves, snap them in place, with each child allocated specific ends of specific curtains, and put the seats back in.

The tire-changing drill was much the same, with the younger children hunting rocks to keep the car from rolling, and the older ones getting the spare tire from its case on the side of the car and rigging the jack. Meanwhile, Dad would strip off his coat and prepare to do the heavy work of operating the jack itself.

We never had any first-aid drills, because Dad was a supremely confident driver. But some of us thought such drills would be even more appropriate than the other ones.

Dad actually sought hairpin curves and potholes to test the car's mettle and hear the tires whine. He thought the best highway defense was a dashing offense. He believed that using the brakes, except as a last resort to cheat the Grim Reaper, denoted a craven lack of spirit. He enjoyed the symphony of blowing the Klaxon, tooting the bulb horn, grinding the gears, racing the engine, and shouting "roadhog!" He equated a car with pleasure, a tour with a joy ride, and speed with gaiety, and he liked to pull the hand throttle wide open, and then sit back and let her rip, while grinning in satisfaction or singing a silly, raucous song.

We were all scared to ride with him; and Mother, who was scared to ride with *anybody,* was absolutely terrified. And on top of everything else, she knew there was always the possibility of his having a heart attack.

She'd clutch the newest and usually carsick baby—the Latest Model—to her bosom, hunching her arms, head, and shoulders around and over the child for protection. Meanwhile, she'd mutter over and over again, "Not so fast, Frank; not so fast."

And he'd open the windshield a little wider, for fuller enjoyment of the breeze, which immediately mounted from full gale to hurricane velocity, and reply in hurt tones: "Good Lord, Boss, we're hardly moving! You don't want me to get pinched for delaying traffic, do you?"

Despite Dad's bursts of speed, we never covered much territory in a day because the younger children required so many bathroom stops. For delicacy, these were referred to as "visiting Mrs. Murphy," and sometimes Mrs. Murphy had company twice an hour.

The boys would go on one side of the road and the girls on the other. And since we were all quite modest, we trudged pretty far back into the woods. The result was that it took a little over two days—with night stops in hotels at New Haven and Newark—to drive down the old Boston Post Road to Montclair.

But when we finally tooled up to the house Dad had bought at 68 Eagle Rock Way, the whole trip—hellish as parts of it had been—seemed worthwhile.

Lillie wrote of the family's arrival in Montclair: "Seen as they first saw it, in the fall, with the leaves gorgeous red and yellow . . . it seemed a fulfillment of a vision of the happy land. Dad had been careful not to describe the new home in detail. To keep their curiosity aroused and stimulate their excitement he stopped in front of many an old homestead and asked, 'Well, how do you like this?' . . . When he finally drove up to the place that was to be home, they could only tumble out, almost breathless with the thrill, and start to investigate the house, the garage, the hot-houses, and all the possibilities of baseball fields, gardens, and homes for future pets."

Part of the tumbling out, of course, was abandoning ship, with the comforting realization that you had arrived alive and unmaimed. And what Dad *actually* did, as we came scorching into Montclair, was to locate ramshackle house after ramshackle house. Then he'd pull into the driveway, park in front of the sagging structure, and say, "Well, kids, this is it —everybody out."

And we'd be sick at the thought of having to live in such a hovel, and be wondering how he could have made such a selection, when he'd say, "Wait a minute. I think I have the wrong place. Our place looks just about like this, but this isn't it."

When we finally *did* arrive at our house, it turned out to be quite a mansion. It was a turreted, three-story, wooden structure with fourteen large rooms and a conservatory— built at the turn of the century. The beautifully landscaped four-acre lot also contained a greenhouse, chicken yard, and two-story barn-garage.

Frank had bought the house at a bargain price, because fewer and fewer people wanted places that size any more. Incidentally, the drain which Motion Study research had placed on the family finances was reflected by the fact that a good-sized mortgage came with the house. Also, the staff of servants was cut to Tom Grieves, Mrs. Cunningham, and a part-time gardener.

The house, although really spectacular, was beginning to get just the least bit shabby by the time we moved in—but not so much so as some twenty years later, when we moved out. The same can be said about the greenhouse, which was unfortunately located forty yards behind what was to become home plate in the family ballpark—and Dad was one of those batters who'd often hit three or four loud fouls before he connected squarely or struck out.

There were two big living rooms on the first floor, and Frank and Lillie took one for an office. The barn was converted into a laboratory, complete with darkrooms. Since the business couldn't be operated without assistants, it was necessary for two stenographers and a photographer to join Mrs. Cunningham, Tom, and the gardener on the payroll.

Frank always regretted not having gone to college, and vowed that all of his children would do so. Although he lectured every year at forty or fifty colleges, he continued to feel sensitive about not having a degree himself. And the fact that he wasn't a college man was sometimes subtly stressed by the Taylorites.

So he was immensely pleased when he received an honorary LL.D. degree from the University of Maine, in his native state. He wore his mortarboard and gown around the house for a day or two, while we all called him "doctor." And he had quite a few pictures made by Mr. Clark, his photographer. It was almost as bad as when he had become a major —but not quite. Sometimes he'd hold his hand out for Mother to shake and say, "Dr. Gilbreth, may I present Dr. Gilbreth?"

Frank was even more pleased, though, when the Society of Industrial Engineers made Lillie an honorary member in 1921. This was the first acknowledgment by any engineering group that she had attained professional status. And although women still weren't allowed to be regular members of the engineering organizations—and in fact weren't allowed even to enter some of the engineering buildings—the S.I.E. was one organization whose meetings were open to women.

Lillie was the second honorary member of the S.I.E. The first was Herbert Hoover. The actual ceremony came as a surprise at an annual meeting in Milwaukee. Lillie was called to the platform—just as she had been, nine years before, at the first Conference on Scientific Management—and presented to the audience. She was shy and embarrassed, and when she couldn't think of anything to say, she motioned to Frank to come up front and bail her out. Still astounded and beaming with pride, Frank bounded out of his chair and strode forward confidently.

The old pro of the lecture circuit was glad to come to the Little Woman's rescue. All the way to the platform, he was framing his remarks.

He stood up beside Lillie, who was dabbing her eyes, and he bowed slightly to the audience. He put his arm around Lillie's shoulders, and he opened his mouth, but no words came out.

The audience applauded, and the Gilbreths took their seats. Then Harrington Emerson, who was presiding, remarked all too truthfully, "Well, Mr. Gilbreth, that's the first time I ever saw you turn down an opportunity to talk about Motion Study. Are you sure you don't want to tell us something about how you make your living?" Frank had recovered enough by then to stand up and wisecrack, "Well, from now on I'm going to make it from the sweat of my frau."

The recognition by the University of Maine and the S.I.E. was certainly welcome, but many engineering groups continued to ignore the Gilbreths. When the Federated American Engineering Societies named a seventeen-man committee on the elimination of waste in industry, every appointee was a Taylorite, and Frank was ignored altogether. This was a deliberate oversight, because Frank had done more work on waste-elimination than any other engineer.

Still, the Gilbreths found satisfaction in the job offers they received from industry itself. And the Montclair house, which doubled as an office, proved to be an excellent selection. If Dad wanted to work at night, the office was right there. And if we needed another player for a baseball or touch-football game during the day, *he* was right there. He certainly shouldn't have put the strain on his heart—and often Mother would call from the house for him to take it easy—but he couldn't resist racing down the base paths or into the end zone.

The office was supposed to be out-of-bounds for young children, but this was one rule that wasn't too strictly enforced, because both Dad and Mother liked to have the children around them, and Dad liked to stop his work and make them drawings or toys. As Mother once wrote, when a young child toddled into the office, Dad would usually pull out a board at the top of his desk, park the child on it, and make something like "an alluring drawing in colored pencil of some atrocious face with a long tongue which wagged in a fascinating manner."

And with a couple of strokes of a pencil, he could change a child's tears to laughter.

Sometimes, looking back, those early days in Montclair seemed even better than the good times in Providence. And even when Grandma died, you couldn't be too sad, because she hadn't been feeling well for so long. But she hadn't "humped or scruffed," and she lay straight in her casket.

CHAPTER 14

The Squelcher

Lillie kept urging Frank to travel less, to slow down, and to stay off lecture platforms. And although he occasionally tried to comply, he found inactivity so alien to his nature that he quickly slipped back into his fast pace.

Often he made three or four speeches a week, and he strode the stage with all the dictatorial aplomb of a captain on his own quarterdeck.

Sometimes he'd take me out of school so I could go to New York with him and hear him lecture. This was meant to be a great treat for me, but I'd sit on pins and needles knowing that the captain was going to lash out fairly unmercifully if any member of the audience wasn't attentive. After all, he was getting old and he was terribly out of shape—and there was always the danger that some member of the audience would lash back.

At one lecture I attended, there must have been four hundred people in the audience, but Frank was as relaxed as if he were talking to a small group. The inevitable two late-comers walked down the aisle, talking in low tones, and Frank used his line about, "Now that all the *important* people have arrived, I guess we can proceed." A few minutes later, when there was some whispering, he gave the offenders the one about, "If you two gentlemen with the loud voices have anything important to say, I wish you'd come up here and say it."

During the course of his talk, Frank mentioned the phrase "One Best Way to Do Work" four or five times. When he finished and asked for questions, a heckler who was obviously against the Gilbreth System arose and said: "I don't think there's any such thing as the One Best Way to do anything. It's a waste of time for grown men even to talk about it. Suppose you were to tell us that the One Best Way to get light was from a lantern—and tomorrow Edison invented his incandescent bulb?"

Frank was smiling deceptively at him during his discourse, and nodding as if in encouragement. Then Frank said, "I'll try to get to that question later, if there's time. Are there any other questions?"

There were five or six further questions—all civil—and he answered them. Then, purposely forgetting the question about the One Best Way, he adjourned the meeting.

As people started to file out, the heckler hollered, "Oh no you don't, Gilbreth! What about *my* question?"

Frank snapped his fingers, as if he'd just remembered it. He smiled toothily and hiked up his trousers over his ample stomach. Those who had started to file out sat down again—they didn't want to miss this one. Frank took off his pince-nez, which he wore on a black ribbon, and twirled the glasses around his forefinger until the auditorium was absolutely quiet again.

"Oh, yes," Frank finally nodded. "About your question—I didn't *want* to answer it, it was so silly; but I certainly *can*, if . . ."

"Then, dammit, *do* it!" hollered the heckler, now becoming enraged.

"Well," said Frank in the long-suffering tones of a professor trying to drum something into the head of a dull student, "if I recall, you used the illustration of Mr. Edison's wonderful invention. Do you mind if I answer with an illustration?"

"Answer it any damn way you want to!"

"Surely. Now I'd say that today you yourself have given a perfect example of a One Best Way; of a One Best Way for a man to make an ass of himself."

The audience guffawed, and there was some applause. Frank held up his hand for silence, because he wasn't through yet. "The One Best Way means the One Best Way devised to date. Now maybe next time I speak here," he continued, "someone will get up and ask a question just like yours—and then bray like this, 'Hee-haw.' Then I'd say that your method had been superseded by something even *better*. The fellow who brayed would have devised a new One Best Way to make a jackass of himself."

This time there was a real roar of applause. As Frank walked down the platform steps, the heckler came charging up to him and shouted, "Speaking of asses, that's where I'm going to kick you. Right in the ass!"

The auditorium became quiet for the third time, and Frank said calmly, "Look, my friend, you're making a mistake. We're all supposed to be gentlemen here. We don't use that kind of language."

"A kick in the ass!" hollered his adversary.

"But if we *did* use that kind of language," continued Frank, who hadn't come up through the building trades without learning something about brawls, "I'd tell you that if there's going to be an ass-kicking, *you* will furnish the ass."

With that punch line, Frank turned his back and made his exit. The unprotected target thus presented may have been tempting—for he still weighed more than two hundred pounds, although the doctors had succeeded in making him lose some weight—but the heckler didn't kick.

Later, at the oyster bar in Grand Central Station, I brought up the subject that we had both carefully avoided.

"Suppose that man had kicked you right in the you-know-where?" I asked—and I was a little embarrassed because I had never before heard my father use a word like that. "What would you have done?"

"That kind never fights, Frank-o."

"Boy, you sure called his bluff, eh Dad?"

"Well, maybe I was bluffing, too, who knows? Anyway, I knew he wouldn't tangle with *us*. Two against one."

"Aw," I protested, "I probably couldn't have helped much."

"You couldn't?" He rumpled my hair. "*Sure* you could. When I walked out of there, I figured you were my rear guard. No one likes to kick a man when his young son is around."

"And besides," I pursued the matter, relishing it, "if there was going to be a you-know-what kicking, he was going to furnish the you-know-what, eh Dad?"

"Right. But now I want you to forget that you ever heard that word. And don't mention anything about it to your mother, Frank-o. She can't *stand* that kind of language."

On another occasion in New York, Frank's talk followed

one by a Taylor man, and the inevitable debate shaped up between Taylor's Time Study and Gilbreth's Motion Study. When the Taylor man finished his speech, the chairman congratulated him and indicated complete agreement with his views. Then he introduced Frank.

"I'm reminded," said Frank, in a voice of sweetness and light, "of a story about a teacher who asked a boy, who was one of her pets, to give a definition of a lobster. And the boy replied, 'A lobster is a red fish that swims backwards.' Well, the teacher smiled and said, 'That's very good, Johnny. You are quite right, except that a lobster is not really a fish; he doesn't swim at all; he doesn't move backwards; and he isn't red until he's boiled. But in every other respect your definition is perfect.'"

Once during a speech in Germany about the waste of motions and materials in industry, Frank saw he wasn't getting through very well to his audience. Suddenly, he lobbed a handful of coins into the middle of the auditorium.

The Germans were startled, and then some of them got down on their hands and knees to seek the money.

"You see," Frank beamed, "you are all shocked by this waste of a few coins. But you don't pay any attention to the enormous waste going on around you. Why, you are wading knee-deep in waste, but you don't recognize it!"

In another speech, Frank was explaining scientific management at an annual meeting of the American Federation of Labor, in the ballroom of the La Salle Hotel in Chicago. He drew an organization chart on a large blackboard and explained the function of every employe. When he was finished, his chart resembled a diamond, with the general manager at the top, the individual worker at the bottom, and the foreman, superintendent, and assistant manager in the middle.

Frank then went to sit beside Lillie on the front row, while the labor delegates gave him a standing round of applause. But the whole effect of his talk was suddenly ruined when Emma Goldman, the well-known anarchist, leaped up onto the stage, pointed at the diagram, and shouted dramatically: "Shame on the Gilbreths! Look at the load the poor workingman is carrying on his shoulders. This is the reason labor is against management. Everyone is on the back of labor."

There was an embarrassed silence, and Frank looked helplessly for a moment at Lillie. Then she was seen to whisper in his ear.

Frank arose, climbed the steps to the stage, and walked back to the blackboard, which was sitting on an artist's easel. Bowing to Miss Goldman, he turned the blackboard upside down with a flourish, putting labor on the back of management.

The delegates, most of whom didn't want the image of being associated with Miss Goldman in the first place, roared their approval. And Miss Goldman, who didn't have the thinnest skin in the United States, was nonetheless so disconcerted that she stalked out of the ballroom.

Germany and France both used the Gilbreths' studies to help rehabilitate World War I casualties. And in many ways, European industry seemed to grasp the importance of Motion Study more quickly than industry in the United States. Frank was especially pleased when he was asked by Czechoslovakia to help establish better production methods there. Specifically, President Tomáš Garrigue Masaryk selected him as the American engineer to teach scientific management to industries emerging in the new republic.

Frank's work there was highly successful, and when he returned to New York he outlined to the A.S.M.E. the progress that Masaryk was making. He suggested that the A.S.M.E. recognize this progress by sponsoring an International Management Conference in Prague.

His suggestion was accepted, and the conference was scheduled for the summer of 1924. Naturally, Frank was to have a key part in the program: He was to make the main speech and to preside over one of the sessions. He and Lillie envisaged this as constituting international recognition—after all the difficult years—of the Gilbreth System's basic originality.

But he didn't make it to the Prague convention, because four days before he was to sail to Europe on the liner *Scythia,* he dropped dead in a telephone booth at the Montclair railway station.

He was talking to Lillie on the phone at the time, and when he stopped talking, she thought perhaps he had made a dash for the train. But about fifteen minutes later, a neighbor rang the doorbell, and said a policeman had asked her to break the news that something terrible had happened to the Major.

He died quickly, they told Lillie. Goodness, he didn't even know what hit him. That was certainly something to be thankful for, they told Lillie—wasn't it? And she said it certainly was.

Anyway, he hadn't had to go through another stay at a hospital. How he had hated that Fort Sill hospital! And that business about wanting his trousers near him all the time. Honestly, when you looked back on it it was almost, well, almost funny!

That's the last time I ever saw Mother weep.

She wrote in *The Quest:* "Suddenly, on June 14, 1924,

Frank went, not abroad as he had planned, but 'West' as soldiers go. The Quest of the One Best Way goes on!"

They dressed Frank in his major's uniform for the funeral.

His brain went to Harvard, where a surgeon friend of his wanted it for some sort of experiments being conducted there. In fact, Lillie found in Frank's personal file—no. 7—the carbon of a jocular letter he had typed himself to the friend, a few months earlier, saying, "My hat size is seven and three-eighths, in case you want to get a jar ready."

Then they cremated him, and Lillie and her Aunt Lillian —the one who had studied with Freud and kept squirrels in her house—chartered a little boat and went out in the Hudson. Standing in the bow, Lillie said a prayer and scattered the ashes.

Was Frank really "ahead of his time"? Of course he was, and he was smart enough to know it.

Answering a critic's assertion that the Gilbreths' scientific books were not well constructed, he once wrote that, poor construction or not, and even if the Gilbreth System wasn't completely understood by some critics, he still hoped that "each paragraph will have a helpful idea for the coming generations."

Maybe there's some danger that this book—by stressing such things as Frank's boisterous humor, his lecture-platform antics, and his Motion Study children—will cause some readers to underestimate the real depth and value of his achievements. I'd be crushed if that were the case.

As Lyndall Urwick wrote in *The Golden Book of Management*: * "That the originality of his mind and his total lack of self-consciousness added to the gaiety of life

* London: Newman Neame, Ltd., 1956, p. 142.

should never be allowed to diminish appreciation of his high seriousness of purpose or of the courage, energy, and devotion which he brought to the service of management and society . . . . Frank Gilbreth was loveable as well as laughable and, above all, a real pioneer."

Then comes the inevitable question: If he was a "real pioneer," was Lillie actually a full partner?

Frank himself threw some light on the question, in a letter written February 20, 1920, to his German translator, Irene M. Witte.

"We are working so closely together," he said of himself and Lillie, "that it is impossible to tell which of us writes a book. Therefore, I would like to see my name on [the German edition of] *The Psychology of Management* and Mrs. Gilbreth's name on *Motion Study* and *Bricklaying System.*"

CHAPTER 15

For Men Only

The house smelled of flowers after the funeral, and when the place had been aired you still thought you smelled them.

And what a boy of thirteen couldn't get used to was that there weren't any Dad-sounds in the house any more.

You kept expecting to hear them—the soothing, bass cadence of conversation; the whistling of Dad's call for assembly, when he wanted to talk to all of us at the same time; the contagious deep-down laughter; even the indignant roars. You hadn't realized how much you'd miss those roars and bellows and sounds that nobody else made.

It was hard for me, as the oldest boy, to believe that my Dad wasn't ever going to come creeping bear-fashion into my room again, snarling and taking imaginary, tickling bites out of my neck and arms. And that my Dad wouldn't be there at bedtime to rumple my hair and cuff me—sometimes too hard for comfort—on the seat of the pajamas. Also that instead of having anyone to take my problems *to*, people were going to start bringing their problems to *me*. And everyone kept telling me that now I was the man of the house, and all I could think about was boy-thoughts like my father playing bear.

Lillie was faced immediately with the problem of money. Frank might have been able to arrive naked on Manhattan with two newspapers—and make a suit out of one and sell the other—but she had no such confidence in her own money-making ability.

Her father had died several years before, and had left his share of the Moller estate to his sisters. Papa had known that the Delger fortune would support in luxury his brood in California, and he had thought that Frank was so successful Lillie would never be in need.

Ironically, two of Papa's sisters had moved from New York to Montclair itself—pampered old ladies rattling around in large houses with French maids and liveried chauffeurs. Lillie faithfully called on them at intervals—mainly at her mother's insistence—but they didn't completely approve of our large and uninhibited family, and when Lillie became a widow the degree of approval dropped for some reason to nearly zero.

Grosie stood ready to help. She telephoned and suggested that we all move to California, where Lillie's four unmarried sisters could help take care of us.

Dad's Cousin Jane—the one Grandma and Aunt Kit feared he might marry—had remained single, and now was a successful dentist. Half an hour after the funeral, she took Lillie aside and told her she wanted to adopt our baby and her namesake, who had just celebrated her second birthday. When Lillie wouldn't agree, Cousin Jane implied that she thought it was selfish for someone with eleven children to take that attitude, especially when adoption would mean that our Jane would be reared with all the "advantages" of an only child.

During the next twenty-four hours, several old friends also offered to adopt some of our children. And when Lillie declined with thanks, they said they'd at least like to become godparents, and pay the children's way through college.

But Lillie, who up until recently had never given money a thought, wasn't prepared to accept charity yet. Also, although a good many decisions had been made for her in the past—first by her mother and then by her husband—she was now making them for herself.

Consequently, she asked herself a question she was to pose scores of times in the years to come: "What would Frank have wanted?" And she knew that the answer was first to keep the family together and second to work for the acceptance of the Gilbreth System and its creation of Happiness Minutes for workers and the handicapped.

So the day after she and Aunt Lillian went out into the Hudson to scatter Frank's ashes, Mother called a meeting of the Family Council. She was pale, and the nervous strain had caused a slight rash to break out on her cheeks. But it seemed natural now for her to be sitting in Dad's chair as the Council's chairman. Anne, a sophomore at Smith College, had moved to Mother's former place, at the right of the chairman; and Ernestine, who had graduated a few days before from Montclair High School and was going to Smith, had moved into Anne's place at the left.

Mother told us about Grosie's suggestion that we move to California, and about the offers for adoption. And then she added that if we thought we could run the house without her on occasion, she could try to carry on the business.

She explained that if she were to take over the business,

she'd have to sail the very next day on the *Scythia* to make a talk at Prague and then preside over one of the sessions of the International Management Conference.

The Family Council voted that she should go. Both Anne and Ern said they'd also stay home from college next autumn and help run the house, but among the decisions Lillie had made before the meeting was that each of her children would graduate from college. So she turned down the girls' offer.

Anne, as the oldest, now thought it was necessary, for the first time in her life, to give her mother a piece of advice.

Taking Lillie aside after the Family Council meeting, Anne pointed out that neither Lillie nor Frank had wanted to mention Mary's name after her death, and instead had kept their grief inside of them, to themselves.

"Let's not do that about Dad," Anne urged. "Some of the younger children won't remember him, and they won't even know what he was like, if we do that. Instead of not talking about him at all, we ought to do just the opposite."

Lillie thought it over and agreed.

"It may not be easy at first," Anne added, "but it will get easier every day."

"I'm sure it will," said Lillie. "And—thank you, dear."

The Society of Industrial Engineers sent a message of condolence to Lillie, and after her talk with Anne she went out of her way to mention Dad by name in her reply.

"I sail tomorrow to do what I can," Lillie wired the society. "It helps me most that you all loved Frank so."

Mother didn't want any of us to go into New York and see her off for Europe, so we all stood on the front steps, along with Tom and Mrs. Cunningham, and waved good-bye. She was sitting in the back of a taxi, wearing widow's weeds, and her eyes were dry—at least they were as the cab pulled away. We wondered whether she'd still be all right when she arrived at the Montclair railroad station and had to pass the telephone booth where Dad died.

A couple of hours after she left, I came down with chicken pox. And within forty-eight hours, all eleven of us had it. Then things went from bad to worse, and the five youngest came down simultaneously with measles.

Anne felt pretty sick herself—but knew that the five youngest felt even worse. She had Tom move all our beds into two large adjoining rooms, so that we could all suffer together while she kept an eye on us.

The older girls then composed parodies of songs, which we sang endlessly when we felt well enough. I remember that one of them, to the tune of "The Monkey and the Weasel," went:

> All around the Gilbreths' house
> The children have the measles
> Sure they itch but we-e-e won't scratch
> Or pop go the measles.

Another, to the tune of the "Limehouse Blues," concluded with the couplet

> I'd like to know where they think we can go
> When all of our spots seem to multiply so.

Anne saw to it that in our letters to Mother no mention was made of what she called the "double-dip epidemic," and invented imaginary picnics and household projects for us to write about instead.

Finally, though, the last rash and pock disappeared, and Anne supervised our trek by passenger steamer from New York to New Bedford, Massachusetts, and New Bedford to

Nantucket—along with two dogs, two canaries, and the gold-fish. All went reasonably well for the remainder of the summer. At least there weren't any further plagues. True enough, I fell off the roof of our Nantucket cottage and broke an arm, and two of the younger children stepped on nails, but no one drowned, was murdered, or starved to death.

Lillie's talk in Prague received splendid write-ups, and the session over which she presided went smoothly. But when she returned from Europe she was terribly disappointed and downright frightened to find that virtually every client of Gilbreth, Inc.—Frank's and her consulting firm—had given notice they wouldn't renew their contracts.

The notices were politely phrased and often quite sympathetic. But the gist was that engineering was a man's world, and they couldn't risk having a woman—no matter how competent—upsetting their factories.

Lillie had expected some of this, when it came to finding new clients. But she had thought of existing clients as personal friends who knew her capabilities, and she had counted on the revenues to defray household and office expenses, and to send the children to college.

To make matters worse, some of Taylor disciples saw in Frank's death an opportunity to speed the death of the Gilbreth System as well. The first indication of this was Frank's obituary in the Taylor Society *Bulletin,* which seemed to be almost a calculated insult. The write-up didn't mention a word about Frank's work, and implied that his sole claim to fame was that he had had the foresight to establish the Taylor Society itself, to honor the great Dr. Taylor. "The Taylor Society is therefore a monument to Mr. Gilbreth's vision and energy," the obituary concluded.

A few months later, the *Bulletin* republished statements Taylor had made fourteen years before, giving himself and Sanford Thompson full credit for Motion Study.

Almost simultaneously, a book by various pro-Taylor contributors called *Scientific Management Since Taylor* was published, and contained no mention of the Gilbreths. Then the Taylor Society brought out a 501-page book entitled *Scientific Management in American Industry,* and it devoted eighteen lines to the Gilbreths.

By nature Lillie was anything but a fighter, and she detested controversies. But at the same time she didn't propose to sit back and see the Gilbreth System buried, while Frank's pioneer work was claimed by somebody else. So she made up her mind that somehow or other, and short of fighting, she was going to keep the system out in the open where eventually it would be recognized.

When word got out that clients weren't renewing their contracts, now that Lillie was president of Gilbreth, Inc., several management consultants offered her jobs within their organizations. But she knew that if she accepted any such offer her loyalty would have to be to her employer, and she'd have to forget about the Gilbreth System.

One of these consultants, Wallace Clark, was a close personal friend, and when Lillie told him why she felt she couldn't work for him or anyone else, he offered whatever help he could give. He added that if she hoped to be recognized in a field monopolized by men, her first goal should be membership in all the important engineering and management organizations to which Frank had belonged.

Lillie already belonged to the Society of Industrial Engineers—having been awarded honorary membership on the occasion when Frank, for once, was speechless.

Frank had wanted to nominate her for membership in the

A.S.M.E., which was really the key group, but had heard through the grapevine that he might as well spare himself the embarrassment, because some of the older members would vote against any woman.

Mr. Clark offered to sponsor her for membership, and pointed out that perhaps the old-timers would feel differently, now that Lillie was a widow trying to make a living. But although she believed wholeheartedly in women's rights, she would rather have gone through the floor than force herself into a place where she wasn't welcome. So she thanked Mr. Clark but said she wasn't willing to elbow her way in.

However, remembering his advice about being associated with professional groups, she accepted an invitation to speak at a dinner in New York welcoming Baron Shiba, a foreign industrialist who had come to this country to observe management techniques. She was in the Midwest when the invitation caught up with her. After completing a talk there, she took the sleeper home, dressed in evening clothes on the train, and rode a taxi in the rain to the University Club.

When she dashed through the front door to get out of the rain, a uniformed attendant grabbed her by the elbow and said, "No you don't, lady."

"Don't what?" Lillie asked.

"You can't run by me like that, ma'am. You know ladies aren't admitted."

"I didn't know," Lillie stammered. Then she added, "What shall I do? I'm the *speaker.*"

"At the University Club?" he chortled. "If you are, lady, I'm Fanny Brice. This club is for men only."

And he put her back out in the rain, where, New York fashion, there weren't any cabs.

Lillie vowed she'd never put herself in a position like that again. But a few months later, she was invited to represent the Society of Industrial Engineers at a breakfast meeting at the Engineers' Club. She had attended meetings there with Frank, so she knew women were admitted. But what she didn't know was that they weren't admitted for breakfast. This time, she already had taken her seat with the committee in the dining room when, after a whispered conversation between the manager and the committee chairman, she was told she had to leave.

Writing to her mother about the rebuff, Lillie eventually was able to see the bright side of the picture. At least, she told Grosie, this time it wasn't raining cats and dogs, and she didn't have on her best dress. "I suppose I can't expect *everything* to go well," she added. "As Frank used to say, 'What success did God get with the Ten Commandments?'"

Meanwhile, as financial troubles mounted, there were the everyday problems of Lillie's new role as head of the family. Anne transferred from Smith to the University of Michigan, where, like Lillie, she became a Phi Beta Kappa. Ern went to Smith. Mart took a postgraduate year at Montclair High School, to help run the family, before going on to New Jersey State College for Women.

The process charts in the bathroom and other strict matters of routine were slackened, because Lillie simply couldn't be strict herself, and never had believed in regimentation, anyway. Instead there was an informal buddy system, under which each older child was assigned a younger one, and made responsible for such things as seeing he did his homework and took his baths.

Incidentally, when Anne came home on vacation and told the family about making Phi Beta Kappa, Lillie actually yelped in surprise, and threw her hands up into the air in glee. A young sister, whose name I'd better not mention, mistook the glee for anguish and said darkly to Anne, "I don't know what you did at college to make Mother act like that, but I'll surely never do it." Years later, in recounting that story, Lillie used to look with sad affection at the younger sister and remark, "And I can truthfully say that she never did."

When Lillie was home—and looking back it was the days she was there rather than the days she was away that one remembers—she herself helped with the homework. Engineer or not, she was still better with such subjects as English and Latin than with algebra and physics. And she always arranged her business appointments so that she could attend all class plays, commencement exercises, and those occasions at which one of us would have to make a speech or read the Bible.

After dinner at home, looking thin and wan, she'd play the piano for us, and we'd all sing "Marching Through Georgia," "Clementine," "Over There," and one of Dad's favorites about a bunch of Irish laborers who worked like "hill" on the railroad. Ernestine played the mandolin and Anne the violin, so when they were home we had a regular concert.

Then all eleven of us would go up to Mother's room and sit around her bed while she'd read to us. She thought the most basic training of all, in rearing a family, was to instill an appreciation of good books. Years later, she wrote: "I can take or leave radio, television, the movies. I still feel that the best gift a fairy godmother can put in any child's crib is a love for reading."

While she was reading aloud, one of the older children would massage some of her hair tonic into her scalp, because her hair was already getting thin, and besides it relaxed her.

All of that may sound like a romanticized Victorian novel, or like Lillie deeming it a privilege to pick flowers for Gro-

sie's breakfast tray; but I can't help it because that is precisely the way it was. Not only that, we actually fought to see
who would be the masseur!

If the house was not kept in the apple-pie order that Dad
and Grandma had insisted upon, that didn't disturb Mother.
Although she admired house-proud women, she didn't propose to be one herself, especially since she had more important things to do. Keeping a spotless house, she used to say,
was like putting pearls on a string with no knot at the end.

So the taut ship to which we had been accustomed became
more easygoing and relaxed. When Mother kept order at all,
she did it subconsciously. Her "I don't believe I'd do that,
dear," was every bit as effective as Dad's "Cut it out or I'll
knock your block off."

Unlike Dad, she didn't rely on either rewards or discipline. But she knew what every one of her individual children wanted, needed, dreaded, and dreamed about. And
when a child talked to her, she listened and listened, and
made sure she understood.

CHAPTER 16

Tom and the Lecture Circuit

Although stressing the need for economies, Lillie didn't let her children know how desperate her financial affairs had become. After all, she had never had to worry about money as a child and, if she had her way, neither would her children.

The college expenses were high, and so were those of the office and laboratory. As Frank's insurance dwindled, she let the photographer and stenographers go. When Mrs. Cunningham, the cook, became ill and decided to go back to Providence and live with her daughter, she wasn't replaced —and little Tom Grieves took over her duties. When the gardener quit, he wasn't replaced either.

We sold Foolish Carriage to a secondhand-car dealer. And although none of us knew about it until years later, Lillie sold back to Tiffany's all of the jewelry—except her wedding and engagement rings—Frank and her father had given her through the years.

But even after those drastic measures, she still had to borrow money from her mother on several occasions, to meet mortgage payments and current expenses.

As for Tom Grieves, he did his best to fill in for Mrs. Cunningham, but the job was just too much for any one person, and besides he was a terrible cook to begin with, and an even worse ironer.

Tom kept a soggy-tipped Sweet Caporal cigarette between his lips from the time he lit it until he spit it out, and the ashes dropped indiscriminately in whatever food he was preparing. His mashed potatoes were lumpy, his meat burned, and his muffins sodden. The laundry he produced was wrinkled, musty, and haggard.

But how he managed to do the shopping, cook three meals a day, do the laundry, cut the grass, rake the leaves, tend the furnace, do the painting and other handyman chores, train the domestic animals, teach the wild birds to light on his hands and the wild squirrels to sit on his shoulders—and still find time to get magnificently drunk two or three times a week—remains a miracle in Motion Study.

Of course the boys helped with the outdoor work and the girls with the housework. And we all felt sorry for him because of his failing health—or what we thought was his failing health.

"Christ, I'm sick!" he'd often moan in the mornings, as he'd stir the muffins, while the smoke from his Sweet Cap went up his nostrils, causing a hacking cough which flipped ashes into the batter. *"Christ, I'm sick!"*

Since Tom did most of his boozing away from home—in the nearby town of West Orange—we weren't aware of the fact that his morning sickness was fortunately ephemeral, and would disappear as soon as he could get back to West Orange, to do the shopping and to obtain what he described as "a little smile."

Tom occasionally would take me with him to West Orange, and he'd leave me in the grocery store, while he disappeared until his smiles became all but hilarity. Although he was diminutive and not exactly what was known in those days as an Arrow Collar ad, the old floozies and the female cooks from other Montclair houses flocked around him. He literally beat them off—with sound smacks on the rear—and occasionally pinched them off, too.

"I like 'em with a little meat on their bones, Frankie-boy," he'd tell me loudly, for their benefit, "like this one here." And he'd spank a prancing two-hundred-pound baby-doll of about fifty summers. "Mum's the word, now, boy. Don't say nothing to your mother. Or this-here one. (Crack!) Or this baby-dumplin'. (Smack!) Sorry, honey—I thought you was one of my dear friends."

No matter where we were in West Orange, if either he or I had to go to the bathroom, Tom would walk into the nearest store—whether he'd ever been there before or not—and ask to use the facilities.

If the clerk so accosted were wise, he would show us quickly and politely to a bathroom. If he should reply that there weren't any such facilities, Tom would flex his fingers into fists and inquire, "Where do *you* go?"

Although he was short and trim, Tom had forearms like the human oxen Dr. Taylor used to study in his experiments with pig iron, so we were almost invariably escorted to the facilities without further ado.

Sometimes on the walk home through the West Orange woods, with grocery crates on his shoulders, Tom would burst into one of his favorite songs:

"When you see a white cat, shave him, shave him . . . When you see a yellow cat, shave him, shave him . . . When you see a black cat or any cat at all . . . Chop off his whiskers and nail them to the wall."

"East is East . . . West is West . . . Now who stole my coat and vest?"

"Frère Jacques . . . Frère Jacques . . . So are you . . . So are you . . . Bring on the Wheatena . . . Bring on the Wheatena . . . Ding dong ding."

"Sur is pont . . . d'Avignon . . . Bring on the pea soup . . . Bring on the pea soup."

The songs that started in French were, of course, Tom's special version of some of our language records.

Tom was quick and tough and practiced what he preached, which was a splendid triple-negative: "Don't never take nothing from nobody."

He could juggle knives like a professional, especially when he was sober; put a cigarette in one ear and make it come out the other; and close his eyes and then walk miraculously to a hopelessly lost object that you'd been looking for endlessly.

Tom was firm in one belief—and we ourselves, however reluctantly, saw the wisdom of it. The belief was that any child who thought he was too sick to go to school needed castor oil. Tom personally mixed the medicine with fresh orange juice in the kitchen. As he came up the back stairs to our bedrooms, he stirred vigorously. The clinking spoon had an effect considerably more dramatic than Pavlov's experiments with his dogs. Not only did mouths salivate, but malingerers hit the deck and genuinely sick children hid in closets. To this day, some Gilbreths can't really enjoy orange juice.

He used to tell wild tales about how, when he was a boy

in Providence, he had a fierce dog who would start the day by killing five or six cats. Yet if anyone now so much as ruffled the fur of one of Tom's cats, the offender would be led out of the kitchen by the ear. He named his various cats for the none-too-complimentary nicknames he had given to the Gilbreth girls: Miss Prim, Teen, Lazy, Smarty, and C. B. The full name of C. B., incidentally, was Tom's favorite cackler: College Bred—Four Year Loaf.

Also, when a young bird would fall out of its nest or break a wing, Tom would chew up toast and feed the bird mouth-to-mouth fashion.

Oh, yes, and he could eat a whole banana under water, too.

Tom eventually took the pledge—but not until all of us were pretty well grown—and lived to a mellow old age. When he finally became too old to take care of himself, we put him in a nursing home, where he proceeded to train the squirrels, birds, and even the nurses. When we visited him, we found he was getting fat and now spoke continually the way he used to when Mother was in the room—good gracious and mercy me had replaced a really masterful command of profanity.

When he finally died, there was some discussion about the ultimate disposal of his ashes. One ghoulish sister-in-law, who had often been a house guest but who failed to appreciate any of Tom's better traits, remarked that while she meant no disrespect for the dead she thought it would be fitting to divide the ashes impartially between the corn muffins and the mashed potatoes.

Tom may have had his share of frailties, but Lillie couldn't have gotten along without him as she took over

Frank's lecture schedule and was away from home much of the time.

She received an honorarium for some of the speeches and travel expenses for almost all of them. In many cases, the travel expenses were a flat fee, regardless of the distance, mode of transportation, or hotel accommodations. So unlike Frank, who always traveled first class and stayed at the best hotels, Lillie rode in upper berths and on buses and stayed with friends. Luckily, she now had friends on almost every college campus. Also, there was a whole army of people, like the nurse at Fort Sill, with whom Lillie had kept in touch through the years. She didn't mind writing them and asking if it would be convenient for her to spend the night. And they seemed delighted to have her. Actually, even in the days when she had plenty of money, Lillie always preferred a friend's home to the impersonality of a hotel.

Lillie would often take along a load of our clothes to darn and sew buttons on, during her intervals of unavoidable delay. At first her sewing left a lot to be desired, but she finally became more skilled. She also took up knitting, crocheting, and handkerchief-making and napkin-making. At meetings and conventions—and sometimes even on platforms where she was waiting to be introduced—she kept busy with the handiwork which often became birthday or Christmas presents for us and for the people whom she had visited. Some years later, when Argyle socks were fashionable, she became quite good at knitting them, and had a waiting list of requests for special color combinations from her sons and grandsons. She made her last pair when a grandson asked her to make a matching pair for his girl. *That* was the limit.

When Lillie first embarked on the lecture circuit, she was so nervous that her face broke out with that troublesome rash again. But as she kept at it, she became a real expert, and actually enjoyed it. She seldom needed notes, she could gear a talk to a specific audience, and she had the unusual ability of being able to sense when she had talked long enough. Also, she had a knack of using personal and faintly humorous incidents to lighten otherwise heavily technical portions of her speeches.

"In our family," she'd say, "we make a game out of Motion Study and we all try to see how we can cut down our own motions. This is especially important in the mornings when you have seven or eight children to get ready for school. One of my young sons insists he could improve his efficiency by at least fifty per cent, if we would eliminate baths and re-place the back stairs with a fireman's pole. And a young daughter who has the job of setting the breakfast table says the One Best Way to do her job is to have everybody go out into the pantry and get his own dishes and silver. Her suggestion, which was rejected by a ten-to-one vote in our Family Council, bears out what our cook and handyman says about us, I fear. He says the Gilbreth System is to get every-one else to do your work for you."

While she was on the lecture circuit, Lillie made a point to walk at least a mile every day, and she also did a brief schedule of setting-up exercises, which Frank had devised for her years before.

She also wrote a collective letter every day to the family at home, and individual letters every day to the girls at college. Her letters were of necessity brief, and always written in longhand. Both she and Frank had adopted an efficient style of handwriting, free of curlicues, which enabled her to dash off a letter in a little over a minute. If her writing happened to be jiggly, you'd know that your letter had been written while she was on a train or bus—and you'd picture her with her briefcase in her lap, forming a table; her sewing bag at one side with a couple of knitting needles protruding; and a stack of finished letters at the other side. Incidentally, she used post-office envelopes with stamps printed on them, and sometimes postal cards. She said you'd be surprised how many therbligs it took to get a stamp out of your pocketbook, lick it, and put it on an envelope.

Her letters were invariably cheerful to a plateau just below ecstasy, partly because she didn't want us to worry about her or money, and partly because that was the way she tried to face the world at all times, and particularly when the going was roughest.

The people she'd mention—usually her hosts—were invariably kind, appreciative, intelligent, and handsome. Even if she had met Old Beelzebub himself on one of her trips, I don't think she would have criticized him in a letter home. She either would have reported on what a quick mind and useful little hoofs he had, or left him out of the letter altogether.

For some reason, too, Lillie always assumed that her family, to the last child, was as intimately acquainted with her far-flung friends as she was herself, although as often as not we didn't know them from Adam's proverbial house cat.

"Dear Family," she'd write, "I had such a lovely stay with Ellen and Fred Martin, and the two talks at Penn State and the Women's Club went well. I think your father would have been pleased. Ellen is so pretty and such a good cook. Ambrosia! Fred should get his full professorship next fall, now that his cataract has been removed. You ought to see how little Freddie has grown. Such blue eyes. I arrive at Lafayette this afternoon for three talks there, and dear Mary Phillips has promised to meet me. Love, Mother."

I was always glad when she had three talks scheduled at a

particular place, because she and I had a special arrangement under which I'd get a share of the honorarium—if there was one—from the third talk.

At that time, the one thing I wanted more than anything in the world was a sailboat, so that my brothers and I could race our own boat, instead of crewing with somebody else, in the Nantucket Yacht Club's regattas for children. And if in retrospect that seems like a selfish luxury for the oldest son of a widowed mother, Lillie thought that each child was entitled to at least one goal of self-indulgence.

So I had an account at the Montclair Savings Bank in the name of the "Frank B. Gilbreth, Jr., Boat Fund." Mother, who had similar arrangements with the other children, would give me ten dollars to deposit every time there was that third honorarium.

It's digression, but good for my conscience, to report that the very next summer the Nantucket Cottage Hospital raffled off a catboat of exactly the class I coveted. For every book of raffle tickets that a volunteer sold, he himself received a free ticket. I worked industriously selling the books, acquired fifteen or twenty free tickets, and won the raffle.

I've never been sure whether the moral of that little success story is that if you work hard your finances will mushroom—or at any rate toadstool—to the point where you can afford your own yacht; or that if you want to live above your means you'd better do some long-shot gambling, like investing a deuce in the daily double. But anyway the Nantucket *Inquirer and Mirror* duly reported that young Gilbreth stepped forward waving the lucky-numbered ticket, with "joy beaming from every freckle." Incidentally, I named the boat *Lucky Number,* and the "Frank B. Gilbreth, Jr., Boat Fund" account was changed, much more practically, to the "Frank B. Gilbreth, Jr., College Education Fund."

Meanwhile, Wallace Clark, who had urged Lillie to seek membership in the professional societies, did some secret and private polling of A.S.M.E. members. He was delighted to find that the opposition to her membership had all but disappeared. Without Lillie's knowledge, he nominated her and she was accepted. This was a real breakthrough, and Lillie was elated when she returned from a lecture tour and heard the news from Clark's wife, Pearl, who was one of her best friends.

Then, equally important, the University of Michigan, recognizing all the effort and time she had spent lecturing on college campuses, made her an honorary master of engineering. This was the first such degree ever awarded a woman by any college, and it couldn't have been more timely insofar as Lillie was concerned. At last there was an answer to those who kept asking what a woman doctor of psychology, who *still* didn't know anything about calculus or much about physics, could offer in the way of credentials as an engineer.

Shortly thereafter, another good friend, Andrey A. Potter, engineering dean at Purdue University, helped her professional acceptance immeasurably by announcing that she would succeed Frank as a special lecturer there. A good deal later, she became a full professor of management at Purdue, the first woman ever to hold such a chair.

But as for landing any consulting jobs in big industries, Lillie couldn't scratch the surface. They'd listen to her tell about the Gilbreth System, in talks at colleges and at meetings of the professional societies; but they wouldn't let a woman come into their plants and install it.

As for the lectures themselves, they not only kept Lillie away from home more than she liked, but also didn't provide the income she needed to run the house, pay college tuitions, and meet the mortgage. So once again Lillie had to borrow money from her mother.

CHAPTER 17

Mother's College

Like many a needy widow before her, Lillie decided to supplement her income by teaching school. Actually, the school was suggested by Robert Johnson, vice-president of Johnson and Johnson, the pharmaceutical firm. He told Lillie his company would like to have one of its own *men* trained in the Gilbreth System, so that there'd be a full-time Motion Study expert on the job, rather than a consultant who would come and go. Mr. Johnson added he realized that Dr. Gilbreth couldn't spend all of her time training just one person, but that perhaps other firms would also like to have their own Motion Study men.

The idea seemed perfect to Lillie, because she could utilize the facilities of the office and laboratory at our Montclair house—and also be with the family. And since her basic aim was the acceptance of Frank's contributions to scientific management, the school offered a splendid opportunity. It was almost like training some "disciples" of her own, and sending them out into industry.

While Lillie was preparing a curriculum and prospectus for her Motion Study Institute, she received a letter from R. H. Macy and Company asking whether she thought micromotion techniques could be applied in the New York department store. The letter led to a conference at which Macy's decided to send a representative to the training sessions.

Not being mechanically minded, Lillie needed someone already trained in the Gilbreth System to run the cameras, cyclegraphs, and projectors, if she were to initiate her course.

Fortunately, she and Frank had kept in touch through the years with Joseph Piacitelli, who had been a young clerk at the New England Butt Company when Frank installed the Taylor System there. It had been partly because of Frank's insistence that Joe had eventually completed his education, and had become an engineer. He was now employed at the nearby Barber Asphalt Company, where Frank had been doing some consulting work shortly before his death. The Barber people agreed to send Joe to the school to run the equipment, if, while there, he and Lillie would work on some specific Barber problems.

So Lillie mailed out the prospectus, and then spent a summer working between lectures as a salesgirl at Macy's, to gain knowledge about the store itself and experience about the fatigue involved in retail sales. She'd come home at night exhausted, and we'd rub her feet and massage her scalp, while she stretched out on her bed and read to us. I guess if she wanted to find out about fatigue, she could hardly have beaten working for a New York department store.

The first Motion Study Institute opened with only three

pupils, including Mr. Piacitelli. The course lasted sixteen weeks, and the tuition was $1,000 a pupil, so Lillie didn't do much more than break even.

Eugenia Lies and William Dorman represented Macy's and Johnson and Johnson, respectively, and when it came to viewing the Gilbreth family, they saw us warts and all. Miss Lies not only had to mediate occasional family fights, but also was fully exposed to Tom. Luckily for all concerned, she didn't have an excess of meat on her bones—so Tom managed to behave himself. As for Joe and Bill, they took recesses every afternoon as soon as we got home from school, and joined us in baseball, touch football, or, if there was snow, building forts and snowballing.

Both men apparently enjoyed their recesses, because Mother and Miss Lies sometimes had to call them three or four times to get them back to the grindstone. I remember on one occasion hearing Bill alibi to Joe, after they had stretched their "break" from twenty to forty minutes, "Lord, you can't concentrate anyway, with all that hollering going on."

"That's right," Joe nodded. "And, anyway, rest periods are an *integral* part of the Gilbreth System, right?"

"Right. Who's at bat next?"

The institute worked out so well, though, that subsequent sessions were much better attended, and pupils came from England, Scotland, Belgium, Japan, and Germany, as well as from American industries. Several of the foreign students started schools of their own when they returned to their homelands. So Lillie had the satisfaction of knowing that Motion Study techniques were being spread around the world.

Also, two of the American firms which sent representatives to the institute—Sears, Roebuck and the Dennison Company—subsequently commissioned Lillie for consulting work. But the type of consulting was a good deal different from the work Frank had done. Sears wanted a survey of its personnel relationships and Dennison asked for a series of lectures on how Motion Study could speed sales. In both cases, it was the human element of management that was being stressed.

After word got out about her assignment for Sears, the president of another large company set up a cloak-and-dagger type of appointment with her in the lobby of a New York hotel. He offered her a fairly substantial fee if she'd make an unobtrusive study of *his* personnel department, and report to him why it wasn't functioning effectively.

Lillie said she'd mull it over. But she phoned him the next day and declined to take the assignment.

"There's really nothing to study," she told him.

"Nothing to study! We've had three different personnel managers in the last eighteen months, and not one of them has been able to make his decisions stick."

"That's the problem," Lillie agreed. "Your heads of manufacturing, sales, engineering, and finance are all vice-presidents reporting directly to you."

"They're the boys who put the money in the till."

"They certainly are. And since the head of personnel *isn't* a vice-president, they naturally don't realize how highly you regard the human relations job."

"Look, Dr. Gilbreth, are you trying to tell me that it's my fault, and that if I really thought the 'human relations job' was important I would have made my personnel manager a vice-president, too?"

"No," Lillie replied patiently, "all I'm saying is that there is no use for a management consultant to try to solve a problem that the president himself could solve in an instant, if he really wanted to."

The next day he sent her a check for the full amount he had mentioned as a fee.

"Mother's College," as we called her Motion Study Institute, continued for six years. Lillie finally ended it when the engineering colleges themselves started offering courses in Motion Study and in other aspects of scientific management, and urged her to help them initiate their new programs. She served as an adviser to a score or more colleges, and was a full professor at Purdue, Newark College of Engineering, the University of Wisconsin, and, later, the University of the Philippines.

Along with her academic work, she was also devoting a good deal of time to rehabilitation of the handicapped. The American Management Association took note of this, in awarding her honorary membership. Then the University of Rutgers conferred on her what she really needed to complete her credentials: the full-fledged degree of Doctor of Engineering.

If there had been any sort of reluctance among the academicians to recognize the achievements of a "woman engineer," the Rutgers degree broke the logjam. Her own University of California, which she dearly loved but which hadn't been able to give her a Ph.D. because of the residency rule, made amends by awarding her an honorary LL.D. Smith College and Princeton University followed. Then, in short order, there were more than twenty others. And newspapers began referring to her as "The First Lady of Engineering."

While she was accepting honorary degrees, working occasionally as a consultant, acting as mother and father to eleven children, winding up "Mother's College," riding upper berths across the country to make lectures, and often donning a Girl Scout uniform to dash to Washington and work with Mrs. Herbert Hoover on scouting, Lillie also found time to write two more books. These were *The Homemaker and Her Job* and *Living with Our Children*. In both, she outlined some of her ideas about efficiency in the home.

Home planning and design was a phase of engineering in which Lillie found a perfect niche. After centuries of drudgery, women were beginning to demand such things as labor-saving appliances and efficiently designed kitchens. Servants were becoming scarce in the metropolitan East. The Irish domestics of Martha's day had long since been assimilated in the Melting Pot, and now their children were themselves homeowners, complaining about the servant shortage. Neither architects nor appliance designers had ever given much thought to the fact that housewives could do-it-themselves if they had the benefit of Motion Study, the elimination of fatigue, and other aspects of the Gilbreth System.

When Lillie started to speak out for efficiency in the home, General Electric and the Brooklyn Borough Gas Company both hired her as a consultant. Also, the New York *Herald Tribune* asked her to help set up its Homemaking Institute, the first of its kind.

The new electric iceboxes which had come on the market were utterly unimaginative. Since no one had given any thought to how an electric refrigerator ought to look, the new models were simply patterned after conventional iceboxes—when really there was no longer any necessity to keep food close to the ice, or to provide such features as the ice chest itself and the drip pan.

Lillie kept saying that the new refrigerators should be designed with the housewife, rather than the iceman, in mind. What refrigerated foods did the housewife use most—eggs, milk, and butter? Then keep them at a level where she wouldn't have to stoop for them. Apply the therbligs— search, find, select, grasp, etc.

And when it came to the new electric washing machines, why should a woman have to get down on her knees and open a valve, and drain the soapy water bucket by bucket? Create three or four Happiness Minutes for ten million American housewives by building a little pump, with a waste-water hose, into the machine.

The appliance manufacturers were eager to know what the housewife wanted. So at last Lillie had found one aspect of industry that would really welcome a woman engineer.

It was ironic that kitchens should have paved the way for Lillie's final acceptance as a management consultant, because through the years Lillie and kitchens had been natural enemies. She hated them and they retaliated. Stoves burned her, ice picks stabbed her, graters skinned her, and paring knives cut her. But necessity had been the mother of invention. On Tom's days off, she had learned how to make creamed chipped beef (which we all, including Lillie, called D.V.O.T., and which everyone *but* Lillie knew stood, rather inelegantly, I must concede, for Dog's Vomit on Toast) and a coffee cake which, while hardly mouth-watering, was at least edible, especially after you learned to cut off and throw away the charred lower crust.

Our girls weren't the best cooks in the world, either. Still, we all became vitally interested in the new projects of kitchen and appliance designs.

After supper, when Tom had finished cleaning the pots and pans, and our girls had done the dishes in the butler's pantry, we'd all descend on Tom and his kitchen. While Mother sketched diagrams on a lined pad, we'd move the stove, icebox, and tables around the kitchen, while we tried to make an imaginary cake with the minimum of steps, stoops, squats, and reaches.

"If we put a worktable on wheels, like a tea wagon," Lillie explained, "the cook could push it in front of her and make one trip into the pantry for all her dry materials, and one trip to the icebox for wet materials."

"Some people," muttered Tom, who didn't enjoy the spectacle of his kitchen being torn up, "don't hardly know a goodness gracious dry material from a mercy-on-us wet one. Who's going to clean up my kitchen when all the bless-Pat Motion Study experts leave?"

Yes, he was always mighty careful with his profanity when Mother or any of the girls were around. He had great respect for Mother and felt a real responsibility for the family since the Major's death. But that didn't mean he was forgoing his right to complain.

"Now that so many people have an electric refrigerator instead of an icebox," Lillie continued, ignoring Tom's question, which she deemed rhetorical anyway, "it doesn't have to be in the back entranceway any more. It can be right up here by the stove. Now let's count how many steps a cook has to walk, from the beginning to the end, to make a cake."

When the experiments were finished, Lillie was always careful to rearrange the kitchen just the way Tom liked it. But that didn't appease Tom. And he was such a talented artist at griping that I used to like to linger behind, after the others had left, and savor the rolling, profane excellence of his laments.

" 'So many people' may have an electric refrigerator instead of an icebox," Tom howled, "but in this house we still got the icebox, for Christ sake. In every other Goddam kitchen in Montclair, they got the kind of brand-new refrigerator that, when you open the door, a little light comes on like magic, for Christ sake. But poor old faithful Tom—he's still got the same Goddam kind of icebox that the Goddam Pilgrim Fathers had to use, for Christ sake. Lincoln freed the slaves"—and this was his favorite observation—"all but one, all but one."

It was true that we hadn't been able to afford an electric refrigerator. But when we finally *did* get one, Tom saw it as a device aimed at separating him from his friends.

Actually, Tom's kitchen was always teeming with company, even though we lived on the outskirts of town. The iceman, milkman, garbage man, ash man, coal man, mailman, and expressman were all bosom cronies of his, and it was standard operating procedure for them to drop into the kitchen where Bunker Oats Were Free. Tom kept a pot of coffee on the stove for them, and perhaps it was occasionally laced with a "smile." And they had sandwich-privileges.

Tom expected some reciprocation for this hospitality, though, and he was adept at getting them to help with various chores.

"Christ, I'm sick," he'd tell them. "Me back is broke, for Christ sake. Give me a hand, will you, and bring the ashes up from the cellar."

And the point is that when we finally got our refrigerator and thus didn't need ice to be delivered any more, Tom complained that the whole business was a deliberate plot to keep the iceman from calling.

"Around here you can't even have a personal friend in for a little demmy tassy, for Christ sake," he'd tell me. "I have to put up with you little bastids all day long, and I can't even take time out for coffee with a friend, for Christ sake. Lincoln freed the slaves. All but one."

Lillie's plans for model kitchens—while admittedly not even vaguely resembling the gymnasium-sized relic at our house over which the only surviving slave presided—were an immediate success. Many of the plans were published in newspapers and magazines, and some of them were made into actual kitchens by various appliance and utility companies, so that housewives could visit them and see how "aisy" it was to work hard.

Besides placing the appliances scientifically in a kitchen, Lillie also saw to it that shelves, sinks, and tables were at a proper height for minimum fatigue.

The magazine articles often were illustrated with photographs showing Dr. Lillian M. Gilbreth, the Motion Study expert, in one of her model kitchens. She always looked cool, collected, and efficient in a cook's smock, and was obviously whipping up something mighty tasty, although you couldn't tell whether it was her famous coffee cake or D.V.O.T.

A customer's booklet describing a kitchen she developed for the Brooklyn Borough Gas Company and Abraham & Straus, a Brooklyn department store, concludes with the poem:

MY KITCHEN
Here I may be a Scientist
Who measures as she makes.
Here I may be an Artist
Creating as she bakes.
Here busy heart and brain and hand
May think and feel and do.
A kitchen is a happy place
To make a dream come true.

The booklet adds that "Dr. Gilbreth, the internationally famous industrial engineer," was able to reduce by five-sixths the number of motions required to make coffee cake; in that particular model kitchen.

When we installed our new refrigerator, Lillie thought it would be good for business—and good for Tom—if she had the whole room remodeled into a Motion Study kitchen which she could show to visitors. But Tom drew the line, and since he couldn't be too articulate around Mother he appointed me as his intermediary.

"Hell, I ain't going to be cooped up like a beejeezeley, sweet-smelling, bobbed-haired housewife, pushing a Goddam worktable around like I was serving tea," he exploded. "Tell your mother I'm a *chef,* not a Goddam female cook, for Christ sake. And another thing—that new refrigerator ain't worth house-room. When the light comes on as you open the door, it scares hell out of my cats. And the ice ain't no good for, well . . . it ain't no good for iced tea."

I duly relayed this to Mother, and the kitchen was left alone. We kept the refrigerator, but Tom was also allowed to keep the icebox, so the iceman rejoined the coffee club. And when Mother's friends sometimes teased her about the contrast between her own kitchen and the ones she wrote about, she simply pleaded guilty and said she supposed it was a case of the cobbler's children being the worst shod. After all, almost any explanation was less involved than trying to explain Tom.

The Gilbreth Motion Study Kitchen—also known as the Kitchen Practical—helped pave the way for new consulting contracts, and Lillie's household and business budgets soon were brought into balance again. When Grosie died in California, Lillie's brothers and sisters sent word to her that they would like to forget—or at any rate defer indefinitely—whatever money Lillie might owe to the estate. It gave Lillie a good deal of satisfaction to know, and be able to tell them, that while she appreciated this gesture the fact was that she had already repaid the debts.

But someplace along the line—perhaps it was when she sold her jewelry to Tiffany's—Lillie had lost whatever little pleasure she might once have derived from the ownership of personal goods. So except for her own modest wardrobe, the household expenses, and the needs and education of her children, she had no desire to make money simply for the making.

"Some people get great pleasure out of owning things, and that's very fine for them," she used to say. "But I find that owning things that are worth a lot of money doesn't bring me pleasure at all—just displeasure. You worry for fear you'll be careless and lose them; you worry for fear you haven't locked them up properly and they'll be stolen; you have to go to the trouble of insuring them; and if you're not careful, people who don't have things as nice as yours will envy you. It's not good to be envied. But if you have to be envied, it's better to be envied for what you are than what you own."

If one of her sisters sent her something like an expensive negligee or pocketbook, she'd wait a decent interval—while the present was packed away in tissue paper—and then give it to one of our girls.

"Whenever a person carries a heavy key ring," she once told me, "he also carries a collection of headaches."

Since she really didn't want more money than she needed, she began to spend more and more time working with the handicapped and with the National Safety Council. In later years, Lillie always said that she considered her work with the handicapped to be her principal contribution.

Actually, there are more handicapped homemakers than any other vocational group, and it soon became apparent that Lillie's Motion Study Kitchens could be adapted to their needs.

Applying experience gained in earlier work with crippled soldiers, Lillie designed entire homes for women with heart trouble and other disabilities.

As a consultant of the first homemaking service for disabled women, established at the New York University Medical Center's Institute of Rehabilitation, she showed women how they could keep house in a wheelchair, peel a potato with one hand, make a bed on crutches, and perform similar tasks. Her Heart Kitchen, designed for the American Heart Association, received almost as much attention as the Kitchen Practical.

She also did studies for the handicapped as a consultant for the University of Connecticut, spent more and more time in Washington as an adviser to the Girl Scouts, and undertook a study to increase the efficiency of libraries across the country.

Lillie had known the Herbert Hoovers since the turn of the century, when Mr. Hoover was a mining engineer. Both the Hoovers had graduated from Stanford a few years before Lillie graduated from California, so they had many mutual friends on the West Coast as well as in engineering circles.

Both Lillie and Mrs. Hoover were enthusiastic scouters, and, wearing their uniforms, they began to see a good bit of each other. Also, when the Depression started, Mr. Hoover appointed Lillie to serve as chairman of the women's section of his Emergency Committee for Employment.

I don't know whether the Hoovers knew that Lillie always preferred to stay with friends rather than go to a hotel. But at any rate, from the time of her appointment until Mr.

Roosevelt's election, she usually stayed at the White House whenever she went to Washington, and she sometimes journeyed with the Hoovers when they went to their fishing retreat on the Rapidan River for the weekend.

Lillie "traveled light"—and although her wardrobe was always adequate, it was more frugal than opulent. The White House maids unpacked her tiny suitcase, and Lillie had to search both bureaus at opposite ends of her room to find her slip and stockings.

Sometimes the Hoovers would insist that she stay there a week or so at a time, and of course Lillie would write every day to each of us away from home. I was attending the University of Michigan at the time, and must confess that when the letters started to arrive on White House stationery, I sought to convince my contemporaries that it was Herb himself who was communicating daily and seeking my advice.

Mother's letters from the White House weren't much different from any others. I still have one.

"It's been a wonderful weekend. I've met such interesting people and learned so much. The Fred Ryans, whom I had met in Duluth, are here, too, and she had just become a grandmother and is so happy. Herbert Jr. gets to look more like his mother every day, I think. He is always so thoughtful. What color socks would you like for your birthday?"

Lillie believed that Mr. Hoover was terribly abused, and that Congress should be ashamed of itself for refusing to authorize him to undertake the emergency measures needed to halt the Depression. She believed with all her heart that he was trying to help the workingman. She didn't think the presidency had really changed Mr. Hoover—except to make him more worried. In any event, he could never be anything but a perfect gentleman. Because of protocol, he'd always get on the elevator first when they headed upstairs after supper.

But on the second floor, he'd stand back and insist that his guest go first. "Downstairs, I'm the President, Lillian," he used to tell her. "But up here you're in our home and it's ladies first."

For some reason—perhaps because the thing she feared the most had already happened, so any other fear would be anti-climactic—Lillie lost her dread of automobiles and lightning after Frank died.

Now she found she was perfectly at home in automobiles. And when airplanes began to supersede the ocean liners and transcontinental trains, she felt even more at home on them.

Lillie was at ease and enjoying the twilight one evening, as she rode in a taxicab from Montclair to nearby Jersey City, where she was to make a talk at a supper meeting. She didn't even see a truck which came bearing down from the right and smashed into the cab, tipping it over.

When they finally got her to Mountainside Hospital, just outside Montclair, she was found to have a bruised knee and a badly broken nose.

She wouldn't go into a private room, because she still needed to save the money—although the reason she gave, when we rushed to visit, was that she liked the company of the two other patients.

"Goodness, I'd be much too lonely in a room all by myself," she told us. Then in typical fashion she found the silver lining. "Don't you think I'm lucky—I'm going to get a whole new nose. You know how thin the old one was. I never did like it."

The broken nose turned out to be more serious than Lillie had thought, and the hospital doctors recommended that a certain New York specialist set it, if she wanted to be sure her breathing wouldn't be impaired.

The specialist agreed to come out to Mountainside to set the nose. But when he heard that his patient was in a semiprivate room—and was a widow with a flock of children—he apparently had some doubts about whether he'd be paid. At any rate, his secretary telephoned Lillie at the hospital and asked for payment in advance.

"But it's Saturday afternoon," Lillie protested, "and I don't think I have that much money in my checking account."

"You can write a check and date it next Wednesday, then," said the secretary. "We'll accept that."

So when the doctor came out that Sunday afternoon, Lillie had a check for him in a sealed envelope. He came breezing into the semiprivate, nodded to his patient in her inexpensive and simple nightgown and bathrobe, and asked whether she was ready for the operation.

Lillie was just about to hand him the envelope when a nurse came in with some flowers.

"Some more flowers for you, dearie," she said. "Shall I send these down to the ward, too?"

"How nice," Lillie replied absently, because she wasn't looking forward to the operation. "And will you just put the card in my dresser drawer with the others."

The doctor noticed for the first time that the semiprivate was full of flowers. And the dresser drawer, when the nurse opened it, was full of cards.

"Would you like me to read the card?" asked the nurse.

"Yes, that would be nice."

"Hey! It's from the White House. And it says, 'We're thinking of you. Lou and Herbert.' "

"How thoughtful," said Lillie, still absently. "Oh, here's your envelope, doctor."

"What's that for?" he asked, not accepting it. "Has my secretary been . . . ? Yes, I'll wager she has! She thinks she has to take care of me—we do so much charity work and our expenses are so high."

Lillie held out the envelope.

"There's no rush about that, Mrs.—what was the name?"

"Gilbreth," said Lillie.

"Later, Mrs. Gilbreth. At your convenience, my dear lady."

Lillie felt like making him take it anyway, but after all you can't be too cavalier with a predated check. And besides, although she certainly had conquered most of her fears, she didn't propose to put the doctor's nose out of joint just before he was scheduled to put hers back in.

Lillie subsequently served on Mr. Hoover's Organization on Unemployment Relief, and later on various committees appointed by Presidents Roosevelt, Truman, Eisenhower, Kennedy, and Johnson, dealing with civil defense, war production, rehabilitation of the handicapped, and problems of the aging. But after the Hoovers left the White House she wasn't an overnight guest there again.

Of the First Ladies she knew, Lillie thought that Mrs. Eleanor Roosevelt was the most interesting. And although she sometimes didn't agree with Mrs. Roosevelt, she admired her effort and energy.

Lillie also used to say that she and Eleanor had one thing in common: outspoken mothers-in-law. In fact she thought that Grandma and old Sarah Roosevelt were alike in many ways—and she said that these similarities helped her to understand Eleanor.

As for Sarah's bluntness, Lillie received a firsthand taste of it at a White House luncheon during the Roosevelt regime. Lillie and the President's mother were sitting a seat

apart, and the man sitting between them offered Lillie a cigarette. She declined by saying, "Not now, thank you."

Lillie wasn't a smoker, and I guess old Sarah thought she
didn't *look* like a smoker, because the elder Mrs. Roosevelt
said, "Do you ever smoke, Dr. Gilbreth?" Lillie replied that
she didn't. Sarah said, just a bit too triumphantly, that she
thought Dr. Gilbreth wasn't a smoker.

"So why," Mrs. Roosevelt persisted, "did you say, 'Not
now, thank you,' when you knew very well you didn't want
one now or later either?"

"Because I thought it was polite," Lillie explained patiently, while the man sitting between them squirmed un-
comfortably and the others at the table cocked their ears.

"Well," declared the elder Mrs. Roosevelt, "I don't think
it was especially polite. I think it was downright dishonest."

There was an awkward pause, during which neither
Franklin nor Eleanor came to Lillie's rescue, apparently not
wanting to tangle with the old lady. Lillie, as already noted,
would do almost anything to avoid a controversy. But for
once she let her temper get the better of her and replied,
"Pshaw! You sound just like my mother-in-law!"

This turned out to be just the right tone, too, because old
Sarah burst into a hearty laugh in which Eleanor and
Franklin—and finally Lillie herself—joined. When the
laughter had died down, there was about fifteen seconds of
silence, and then Eleanor gave one final, choking snort and
almost had to be excused from the table.

CHAPTER 18

An Aspirin for Lillie

Anne graduated from Michigan, Ernestine from Smith, Martha from New Jersey State College for Women, Frank from Michigan, Bill from Purdue, Lill from Smith, Fred from Brown, Dan from the University of Pennsylvania, Jack from Princeton, Bob from the University of North Carolina, and Jane from Michigan.

And Lillie's hair changed from red to white, without much of an interval of gray. Now she wrote letters regularly to a score of grandchildren, as well as to her own children, and interrupted her busy business schedule to attend *their* class plays, Bible-readings, and graduation exercises.

She still kept the knack of *listening* to people, and her grandchildren sometimes confided to her things they hadn't told even their own parents.

"God made each of us different from everyone else in the

world," she once wrote. "Because of this uniqueness, we can learn something from everybody. Even from a mentally retarded person, we can perhaps learn how to help him and others; and from a crushing bore, how not to be a crushing bore."

Lillie reached the normal retirement age of sixty-five in 1943, but she was just beginning to get her second wind—and certainly she didn't have the slightest intention of retiring.

To make certain that her mind stayed sharp, she started memorizing a couple of stanzas of poetry every morning. She'd be up at dawn, do the few physical exercises Frank had devised for her, and learn her poetry, all before breakfast. Some time during the day she'd walk her mile, often humming Wagner, which she knew by heart. If there was a break in her business schedule, she'd go to a matinee of a play or musical comedy, often by herself. By nightfall, unless she had a speaking engagement, she was ready for bed. She'd lie down, utterly content, with a book and a few magazines. She slept in snatches, reading in between, and always arose rested and refreshed.

Her health was amazingly good, and she would go literally for years at a time without taking any sort of medicine—even so much as an aspirin, which she thought might be habit-forming, anyway.

Five of her sons—all except one who had slight heart damage from a childhood bout with rheumatic fever—were in the Army and Navy, and spent most of their time overseas. I guess it goes without saying that Lillie wrote each of them every day.

"Why should I retire?" she wrote me on her sixty-fifth birthday, after I had asked about her plans. "Your father and I always believed that compulsory retirement failed to put the health and happiness of the individual worker above the demands of a heartless system. Under the system, the employer gets old people off his payroll and the young employe finds room at the top—so everyone is happy except the retiree!"

She continued on the faculties of Purdue University, Newark College of Engineering, and the University of Wisconsin. President Roosevelt appointed her to the educational advisory committee of the Office of War Information and to the subcommittee on education of the War Manpower Commission. And with war production in high gear, she was in demand as a consultant in various factories.

Among her clients was the Arma plant of Brooklyn, which had an all-male force of several hundred, and which planned to hire eight thousand people—including three thousand women—in a crash expansion program to fulfill a huge Navy contract.

"We've never had women in the shop before," a panicky manager told her. "We don't know how to start. We're counting on you to tell us everything that we have to do to get ready for them."

"If that's all my job is," said Lillie, in what was to become somewhat of a byword in the War Manpower Commission, "I can finish it with this one sentence: 'Build separate rest rooms.' "

Lillie came into Brooklyn two mornings a week, on Mondays and Thursdays, to do her stint at Arma, and always arrived at eight o'clock sharp. But one Monday morning, she hadn't shown up by ten o'clock, and the office staff became worried that something might have happened to her— perhaps on the subway en route to the plant.

A few minutes after ten, Lillie finally arrived, unruffled, with her left arm in splints, hanging from a sling.

"One of my boys got leave from the Navy and spent the night at home," she explained. "So I got up early this morning and rinsed out some of his things. It was still a little dark when I was hanging them up, and I slipped on something and hurt my arm."

"Well, you certainly shouldn't have tried to come to work with a hurt arm," someone told her. "You should be home in bed."

"It was only a hairline fracture," said Lillie, "and I thought we already had enough Monday morning absenteeism here at Arma. Besides I gathered from the doctor that just as long as I didn't jiggle it . . . I'm sorry I'm late."

As Lillie increased in professional stature, so did the realization among the new generation of management people that the Gilbreths had been real pioneers in their field.

Lillie rarely made any claims for Frank, and never for herself. But the integrity of her books, lectures, and work belied earlier assertions by the Taylorites that the Gilbreths were phonies, and that Frank was, as Hathaway had put it, "either raving crazy or a fakir."

Lillie felt that the battle for recognition would never be completely won, though, until such time as the A.S.M.E., which was a sort of quasi-judge of professional ethics, decided of its own accord to make some acknowledgment of Motion Study and the Gilbreth System.

In December 1944 she received what she described as the best news of her life: word that the Gantt Gold Medal for contributions to management would be awarded to Frank, posthumously, and to her at a joint annual dinner meeting in New York later that month of the A.S.M.E. and the American Management Association.

The medal was named for Henry L. Gantt, the one-time Taylor disciple from whom Frank had won a guinea some thirty years before in London, by speeding the production of a little Japanese girl who was working with shoe-polish labels.

It turned out, also, that the presentation was to be made by Wallace Clark, who twenty years before had so kindly offered Lillie a job in his own management firm, after Frank's death.

But if Lillie was excited she didn't show it. Of course she made plans to attend, and even bought a simple black velvet dress for the occasion. Also, she notified her children, so that those who weren't away at war could attend. But on the day of the presentation, she went about her chores as usual in New York.

Exactly an hour before the affair, she arrived at the apartment of Edna Yost, her friend and biographer, to change into her new dress. Lillie had been working hard all day. She freshened up, put on the new dress, and then with only a couple of minutes to spare sank into a chair for a moment's rest.

"Edna," she said, "I hate to trouble you, but I believe I need an aspirin"—and it was one of the few times that anyone ever heard Lillie even imply that she might not feel quite up to snuff, and needed medicine.

The aspirin apparently did its job satisfactorily—and luckily didn't make a dope fiend out of Lillie, either—because she looked very much at ease during the banquet.

At the presentation ceremony, she paid close attention to the citation, as it was read by Mr. Clark, because she hadn't been allowed to see it in advance. She took a deep breath and her face lit up when she heard that the medal was awarded to the Gilbreths "in recognition of their pioneer work in management and their development of the principles and techniques of Motion Study."

Lillie whispered, "Thank you," as applause from hundreds of engineers, government officials, and the military brass and their wives filled the room.

In *Frank and Lillian Gilbreth, Partners for Life,* Mrs. Yost wrote: "No woman ever received an ovation with less self-consciousness than did Lillian Gilbreth that night, feminine and soft in black velvet as Frank would have liked to see her. Walls fell that night . . . . When emotional acceptance replaces fear and antagonism and injustice, human beings have already taken a great step forward."

Subsequently Lillie became the first woman to receive the Herbert Hoover Medal, and this time the citation included mention of her work with the handicapped. It said in part: "She recognized the principle that management engineering and human relations are intertwined . . . . Her creative effort in modifying industrial and home environments for the handicapped has resulted in full employment of their capabilities and elevation of their self-esteem."

Among her other awards were the first Gilbreth Medal, created by the Society of Industrial Engineers, the Wallace Clark Award, the Washington Award, and the Gold Medal of the National Institute of Social Sciences for "distinguished service to humanity."

Yet Lillie used to say that the greatest compliment she ever received was not from any sort of an organization—it was from her youngest daughter, Jane, who at the time was in the third grade. Jane's teacher was asking each child, in turn, what his father did for a living.

"Now Janey," she said, "we know your father isn't alive, so suppose you tell us what your mother does."

"Well, anything I ask her to," said Jane. "Sometimes she irons my party dresses, and she reads to me and helps with homework."

"But Janey, doesn't she have a career?"

"I don't know. If she does, it never bothered me."

Lillie's two goals had been recognition by the A.S.M.E. of Frank's contributions to management and a college education for each of her children. These were accomplished almost simultaneously with the receipt of the Gantt Medal and Jane's graduation from the University of Michigan.

Then Lillie and Jane moved to a third-story walkup apartment in downtown Montclair, and closed the big house at 68 Eagle Rock Way. Since Lillie didn't drive, she had hunted until she found a place that was within walking distance of the retail stores, the First Congregational Church, the train and bus to New York, and the Montclair Public Library, of which she was a board member.

Lillie next called a final meeting of the Family Council, and after some soul-searching we decided to have the old ark torn down. By then, the once stately mansion had become pretty decrepit from the ravages of eleven children and their friends. Also, through the years, Lillie simply hadn't had enough money to make all the necessary repairs. So we couldn't have got much money for the house, even though the lot had become increasingly valuable. And, besides, we simply couldn't envisage any other family living in our house.

But it was a sad decision. And even today, I can walk up the stately front steps at night—in my mind—and into the big front hall, and through the honestly built, hand-paneled house, room by room, and reach automatically for every light switch.

The barn-garage, where the photographic laboratory had been installed and where for a while we kept a flock of Plymouth Rock hens, was left standing. Subsequently it was sold and converted into a charming suburban house, which is still there. Then we sold the main lot, and someone built a new house on it. That was the end of "Sixty-eight" as far as we were concerned.

When Jane married, Lillie had the apartment all to herself. She converted the back bedroom into a small office, with a studio couch to accommodate those of her children and their spouses from out of town who might want to spend the night. It certainly never occurred to her to move in with one of us, although on her lecture tours she managed to spend a couple of nights with each of her children, two or three times a year.

Not wanting to be burdened with valuable possessions, she gave away most of her best furniture, pictures, and china.

"I like to see things being *used*," she'd say when she came to visit and saw some of her presents. "They look so much better here than they even did at our house, don't they?"

In her apartment, she surrounded herself with some of the things she liked best: a few pieces of the furniture Frank had bought years before for his duplicate mothers, including one of the twin mahogany rockers she had first seen in Boston; some pieces Frank had bought especially for her; handmade ashtrays and bookmarks, given to her for Christmas by her grandchildren; and beautiful and often valuable presents—such as crystal from Sweden, porcelain from Denmark, and wood carvings from New Zealand—which had been given to her by various organizations she had addressed or helped.

And she also saved for herself—and began to use whenever she had company—just a few pieces of the beautiful old china she had kept tucked away for fear of breakage while we were growing up.

Every room of the apartment, though, was dominated by books, magazines, technical journals, and correspondence, and Lillie's files gradually overflowed from her little office into the hallway.

Actually, Lillie was traveling much of the time, and when she was home her apartment was usually packed with company. For one thing, Dan and Jack and their families were right there in Upper Montclair, and were in and out of the apartment all day long. Also, Ern, Bill, Lill, Fred, and Bob and their families were in the New York area. To run down the rest of the roll, Anne, Mart, and Jane were on the West Coast, and Frank was in Charleston, South Carolina.

Lillie also had her own group of friends in Montclair—management people, educators, and the town's head librarian. Now that she was free of her homemaking duties she had time to widen this circle considerably.

So if anyone had the idea that the Montclair apartment was the end of the road for Lillie, or that she was going to pine away for her children, he couldn't have been more wrong. Our vanity was shattered to discover that she seemed actually to relish the quiet and privacy of living by herself. And, perhaps because she wanted to be certain we didn't feel guilty of neglecting her, she went out of her way to stress the advantages of being what we used to call, when we teased her, a "superannuated bachelor girl."

"Sometimes it's a comforting feeling," she'd say, "to be able to put something down and know that, when you come back, it won't have been lost, moved, broken, eaten, smeared with jam, painted, or colored with crayons. And, goodness, isn't it a luxury to be able to sit in a bathtub and not worry about whether you've used the last of the hot water, whether

anyone else is waiting to come in, and whether you've remembered to lock the door."

"You sound as if you didn't *like* having a dozen children!"
I once protested.

"Of course I liked it!" she protested. And then with a perfectly straight face she added mildly, "But let's just say, dear,
that occasionally it had its disadvantages."

CHAPTER 19

Queen for a Day

My sister Ern and I wrote *Cheaper by the Dozen* and *Belles on Their Toes* four or five years after World War II. Lillie, who had just been named Woman of the Year by the American Women's Association, agreed to help with publicity by appearing on some radio and television shows with us.

I'm not sure whether Lillie was too crazy about either of the books, because they stressed the comical aspects of raising a big family by Motion Study methods, and she might have preferred that the stress be placed on other, more meaningful aspects. And of course there *was* the danger of allowing humor to eclipse Frank's dedication and the importance of his pioneer work.

But Lillie was pleased, of course, that we were getting the royalties from two best sellers. And I think she believed that, basically, the books did considerably more good than harm in publicizing the Gilbreth System.

Lillie was then in her early seventies. You simply couldn't believe that here was a woman who used to hide from lightning or whose face used to break out in a rash because of nervousness about speaking. Now she was the sort of platform-pro who could cope with anything. You could have shaken her awake in the middle of the night and pushed a microphone in her face—and she could have gracefully welcomed the Shah of Iran to our shores, or accepted the key to the city from the Lord Mayor of New Delhi.

The first television show that she and I went on was a local program in New York, on which the host interviewed a guest or two each day, and gave all the commercials himself. I forget his name, but he was new at the business and, if anything, even more lip-trembling terrified than I.

Before the show, we were led into a little office and had coffee with the host so that we could get acquainted. He hadn't read either of the books, although he made believe he had, but that was all right—you really can't expect TV men to read a book or two a day besides everything else they have to do.

Then we went into the studio itself. In those early days of television, the cues for various programs were written on large blackboards behind the cameras. Our man nervously prepared his blackboard.

He wrote down "Gilbreth" at the top, because he didn't want to have a mental lapse and forget whom he was interviewing. Then he wrote down the names of the books and a few questions we had agreed that he'd ask. And finally, after consulting a director, he wrote down the names of two products he was supposed to advertise.

Then Mother and I sat on a sofa, and he sat on a chair.

We were all given fresh cups of coffee, and he and I lit cigarettes to show how at ease we were. A light flashed, and we were on the air.

The host said he wanted to wish everybody a very pleasant good morning, and that he was pleased indeed on this very beautiful morning in little old New York to have the well-known consulting engineer, Dr.—he checked the blackboard —Gilbreth, and her newspaperman son, Mr.—he checked the blackboard again—Gilbreth, Junior, on his program. He added that Mr. . . . . Gilbreth had just collaborated with his sister . . . Ernestine, and that they had written . . .

His voice had become firm and the fingers clutching his cigarette had been steady, once he was on the air. But then a look of absolute horror came over his face, as a flunky cleared the blackboard with three swoops of an eraser and began wheeling it away. Our interviewer half rose in his seat to protest, and then decided he'd better not let his listeners know that he needed prompting. And as he sat down again, he tipped his coffee over on his trousers, causing a big stain in a horribly embarrassing location.

I was ready to go through the floor right along with him, but Lillie took it in stride.

"Oh, what a shame," she said. She fished into her briefcase and produced a linen napkin she had been making— scalloping the edges and embroidering a monogram. "But, here. Spread this over your lap, and it won't show. I *do* hope it didn't burn you!"

All I could think of to say was, "Me too."

He blushed and said he didn't think so.

"I don't blame you for being startled," said Mother, bailing him out, "because what just happened"—she looked at the camera and smiled—"was that my son and I were a little afraid we might get rattled and forget things, so we wrote a few reminders on a blackboard behind the camera. And *just* as we went on the air, someone must have needed the blackboard for something else, and erased it. But, never mind, we'll get along all right, won't we, boys?"

We both nodded, and by that time the director behind the cameras was scribbling "Gilbreth" on another blackboard, and writing down the names of the two products our interviewer was supposed to tout.

After that, the show went well. When it was over the host thanked Mother for taking the rap for him.

"Not at all," she replied. "And if I were you I'd rush those trousers to the cleaner, because coffee stains are hard to get out, you know. And be sure to tell the cleaner what it is, because otherwise he may not be able to remove it."

I couldn't help but titter, partly in relief that the tense program was over and partly because, in view of where the trousers were wet, I would have bet my last dollar that our interviewer would certainly explain that it was coffee.

"I don't think he'll need a blackboard to prompt him about *that*," I whispered to Mother as we walked out of the studio.

"Eskimo!" she reproved me, but she smiled nonetheless. "That poor dear! I kept thinking that probably his wife was watching—and I felt so sorry for her. And his two daughters, Wendy and Linda . . ."

I deduced that Lillie had been *listening* again.

Not long after that, she, Ern, and I went on Mary Margaret McBride's radio program. Since we weren't on TV and there was only an audience of a few hundred people, Ern and I made a lot of notes before the show, and so did Mary Margaret. But Mother went noteless as usual, and instead produced a partially knit sweater from her briefcase, and worked on it.

Halfway through the program, though, she dug quickly into her briefcase again, found her notebook, and wrote something in it.

"Did you have something in particular you wanted to say, Lillie?" Mary Margaret asked her.

"No, not really, dear," replied Mother.

"Well, we're old friends," said Miss McBride, "and I guess you've been on this program five or six times, haven't you?"

"At least."

"And that's the first time I ever saw you make a note. Do you mind telling the radio audience what it was?"

"Well, it really isn't important," Mother stalled. "And it didn't have anything to do with the children's book."

"Come on, Lillie," Mary Margaret coaxed. "What did you write in your notebook? What thoughts does a famous woman engineer have when she's sitting around a table like this with two of her children, a radio commentator, and a coast-to-coast audience?"

"It wasn't important, dear," Mother repeated. "But if you *must* know, I want to try some of that powdered coffee cream you talked about on the commercial. You see, I'm away from home a lot, and regular cream goes sour. And you made it sound so good, I wrote it on my shopping list. So there you are. I *told* you it wasn't important," she finished lamely.

"Not *important!*" shouted Mary Margaret. "Dr. Lillian Gilbreth, you are an announcer's dream! In fact, that sounded so convincing that I'll bet a lot of listeners think it must have been rehearsed. But it wasn't, was it folks?"

The people in the audience, who worshipped Miss

McBride anyway, all shouted no, Mary Margaret, it wasn't. And Miss McBride told Lillie she wished she had her on the show every day.

Mother was in the audience one night when I was on a program with Richard Kollmar, who had read *Belles on Their Toes* and hadn't liked it. Kollmar and his wife, Dorothy Kilgallen, had their own morning show, so it goes without saying that he was a good deal more skillful and relaxed than I—which is still damning him with mighty faint praise.

"Of course, Mr. Gilbreth," said Kollmar, "everyone is in favor of motherhood. But mothers are human beings, too. The thing I couldn't stand about your and your sister's book is that you made your mother so terribly saccharine. I believe she's got you buffaloed! Has she?"

That wasn't the easiest line I had ever had flung at me, so I temporized by saying that I didn't think my mother buffaloed anybody.

"Nobody could be as saintly as you depict her," he persisted. "She's sitting right out front there. Look at her. Do you mean to tell us that you never saw her lose her temper, or slap one of the kids, or take a sip of wine, or stand in front of a mirror and admire herself, or swear when she cut her finger?"

I looked down from the stage at my mother, but she was crocheting something and didn't raise her eyes. I thought it over briefly. I had *heard* of her losing her temper—once at the Fort Sill Hospital, where Dad was all but dying, and once, moderately, when the elder Mrs. Roosevelt cornered her on not smoking. But I certainly hadn't seen it myself.

"I suppose everybody thinks his mother has saintly qualities," I finally replied. "But I can honestly tell you I never saw any of those things you mentioned."

"And you never saw her," he added skeptically, "so mad inside that she wanted to bite nails? Do you maintain that she just sits up there on the imaginary Mount Olympus where you've placed her, above all the baser feelings that sometimes afflict all the rest of us?"

I told him that I certainly didn't maintain any such thing, and that perhaps she occasionally *did* become mad enough inside to bite nails, but the point was that I'd never seen her bite them—and that she was mighty good at covering up her wrath.

He said plainly that he simply didn't believe me, that he thought saccharine mothers were an anachronism, and that our book had made him, almost literally, sick. I replied in kind that if there was anything that made me almost literally sick before I had had my morning coffee it was bravely cheerful, aren't-we-sophisticated husband-wife shows—or worse yet, wife-husband shows—with canaries singing in the background. I'm not positive that they had canaries on his *Dorothy and Dick* show, but one of the similar morning shows did, so I'm sure he got the point. And I certainly got his point. But what's a child to do—invent vices for his maternal parent? Have her bat the kids around, keep a bottle of vodka in the chandelier, seduce the iceman, and blow marijuana smoke at the damned canaries?

I didn't mention it on the air, but there *was* one occasion when Lillie was mad enough to bite nails, and couldn't quite hide that fact. She didn't lose her temper, but she was so furious her hands trembled and her voice shook—and she was surely at least a country mile below Mount Olympus' serene heights.

Ern and I, with the consent of Lillie and the rest of the family, had just sold *Cheaper by the Dozen* to the movies. We all knew that this was somewhat of a calculated risk—

that Hollywood might change the story around and make the Gilbreths look foolish. And to prevent this possibility, Ern and I did our best to cooperate with the studio officials and men assigned to produce and direct the show.

Most of the Hollywood people we dealt with were, to use the cliché, perfect ladies and gentlemen. But there was one fat studio official who was simply the stereotyped example of Hollywood newly rich vulgarity. And he and Lillie had about as much in common as Mae West and Mahatma Gandhi.

He was one of those soft, pig-pink men with tiny hands and feet. He wore tailored shirts and $400 suits. His little nails were beautifully manicured and his thinning hair was greasy. Also, his jowls quivered every time he took a step. Let's call him Mr. Ward.

I had talked Lillie into inviting him and me to tea in her Montclair apartment. I hoped that if he saw her as she actually *was,* he wouldn't have the nerve to depict her as a *femme fatale* or, worse still, a screwball.

He was staying at the Plaza in New York, where he had a five or six room "soot," and I went up there to meet him, so that we could ride out to Montclair together.

A Filipino butler let me in, and Mr. Ward was wearing a silk dressing gown, finishing a beer, and having his toenails clipped by a cute white-clad manicurist from downstairs. I caught a fleeting glimpse of a negligeed blonde in a distant room.

There was a very large heart-shaped box of candy open on the coffee table. Mr. Ward didn't get up to greet me—partly, I suppose, because the manicurist was cuddling one of his revolting little tootsies. He did, however, have the grace to point to the open box of candy.

"Help yourself, Mister," he said, not taking the trouble to

dignify me with a name of my own. "Go ahead and take a couple—take all you want."

I helped myself. About a quarter of the pieces were gone —with their crinkled paper containers empty in the box.

The manicurist put a sock and shoe on his bare foot, and I didn't envy her. He gave her ten dollars, and told her to get her cute little you-know-what out of there, but to bring it back at the same time tomorrow. He called the doorman to have his "limo" standing by, and fixed his hair with a comb as greasy as George Raft's. Then he grunted out of his dressing gown and put on his shoulder-padded jacket, and we were on our way.

Just as we got to the elevator, he frowned and said, "Say, I forgot something. Does your mother like candy?"

I said that sometimes she did.

"Wait here, then, I'll be right back."

He returned to the "soot" and came out in a moment bearing the big heart-shaped box of candy.

"The box is so big that I guess your mother won't mind if some of the pieces are gone," he said. "Hell, there's still plenty left."

A chauffeur drove us in the limousine through the Lincoln Tunnel and out to Montclair and Mother's apartment. We didn't have much to say on the way out, and I kept wondering what Mother's reaction would be to a secondhand box of candy, regardless of how big. It also developed that Mr. Ward hadn't read our book, but one of his flunkies had read it for him and told him about it—and it was "truly great."

When we got to Mother's, he didn't like the idea of having to walk up three flights. But much as I was trying to butter him up, I didn't offer any piggybacks. I did carry the box of candy for him, though, but I was careful to relinquish it before we entered. I had a distinct feeling it was going to be wise for me not to be associated with that candy in any way, shape, or form.

I rang the bell and Mother let us in. As I've indicated, she had a spacious and comfortable apartment, and despite her age the steps weren't the slightest challenge to her. However, the furniture *was* neither sparklingly new nor pricelessly antique, but instead comfortably worn Victorian. The various appurtenances—such as ashtrays, vases, trays, silver cups, and bowls—had been carefully winnowed by Lillie from hundreds of presents. Some had been made by blind children in India, hospital patients in Mexico, and handicapped women in the Philippines. Some had come from her mother and from Frank. A few were quite valuable, but many had no intrinsic worth at all. Yet each piece meant a great deal to her.

Also, it must be conceded that Lillie's housekeeping, while not quite feckless, would still have had trouble passing a West Point inspection. And the combination of too many books, magazines, technical publications, files, and the appurtenances gave the place a relaxed, cluttered, lived-in look that did not resemble the Plaza.

"I guess," said Mr. Ward, after I had introduced him and he had looked around, "that the family can use the money, eh Missus? Well, can't we all?" He descended cautiously into a comfortable but well-worn armchair covered with striped, dark-green velvet. Years ago, at "Sixty-eight," that chair had always been the caboose, when we laid the furniture on its side and played train.

Lillie didn't know what to say to that, so she didn't say anything. When she poured the tea, I saw she was using some china that had belonged to her Delger grandmother. Mr. Ward doubtless drew a good salary, but it might have surprised him to know what value had been placed on the cup and saucer, now balanced on a fat thigh, when the Delger estate was finally settled.

The coffee cake, as I had feared, was from Lillie's own kitchen and "just like Mother used to make." I peeled off the burned bottom of my piece when she wasn't looking, and slipped it into the wastebasket. The top part wasn't half bad.

Conversation lagged for a while, and then Mr. Ward asked Lillie, "How would you like to come to Hollywood, on an all-expense-paid vacation, and meet some of the glamorous stars?"

"I don't believe I could spare the time, thank you," said Lillie.

"You'd get to see the whole country, coast-to-coast," he said. "Chicago, St. Louis, Santa Fe, you name it."

"No thank you," Lillie said icily.

"And all the movie stars," he continued, gesturing. If he knocked over his cup, I was set to try to catch it before it hit the floor.

"We could get you fixed up like they do on that show *Queen for a Day,*" he said. "Think of it, Missus. Your dreams come true. A dress by Edith Head. Hair and make-up by Perc Westmore and his brother. Maybe a dance with Fred Astaire. And a candlelight dinner, complete with pheasant under glass and wine, with someone like Cary Grant or Spencer Tracy or . . ."

"I'm sure that would be very pleasant," Lillie managed. "But no thank you."

"You don't think I could arrange it, eh? Listen, they jump when I snap my fingers. You scared of airplanes? You can go by train."

"No thank you." Lillie's lips were pursed.

"Maybe," I said, trying to take some of the tension out of the atmosphere, "I could go instead of her. *King for a Day!* Hair by George Raft, shave by Betty Grable, and a wedding to Lana Turner. Then . . ."

"Not you," he grunted, "her. She's good for publicity. You ain't. Dear little old lady from a suburb in the East. Before and after pictures. Get what I mean, Missus?"

"I get *exactly* what you mean, Mr. Ward," Lillie enunciated. "You want to take a little-old-lady who has never been to the big city before and whisk her to Hollywood, the Land of Make-Believe, where she would be magically transformed . . ."

"That's right, Missus," he interrupted enthusiastically. "That's just it. The Land of Make-Believe. Well, what do you say?"

"I say *no*," said Lillie, and it was then that, as I mentioned earlier, her hands trembled and her voice shook.

He turned to me and shrugged. "Well, Mister, I think it was worth the trip out here, anyway. I got some of the atmosphere of the place, know what I mean?"

He moved his cup to a windowsill, and I breathed a sigh of relief. After he arose, he remembered the box of candy, which he had left on a table.

"Do you like candy?" he asked Lillie.

She was too upset to answer. He picked up the heart-shaped box and handed it to her.

"Here, take it."

"Buy yourself a good cigar," I told her, still trying to keep the conversation light.

Upset or not, Lillie couldn't forget her manners. "Why it's beautiful," she said woodenly. "Thank you very much for your thoughtfulness."

"My pleasure, Missus," Mr. Ward said as gallantly as I

guess he ever said anything. "And thanks for the tea. Very tasty. And as for the gingerbread . . ."

"Coffee cake," I corrected him hastily.

"Well, whatever it was, Missus, it was yummy."

Lillie placed the box back on the table, and as she did so the top came off, and you could see all the spaces and empty wrappings. I guess it was hard for her to appreciate the humor in the situation, because the thought of being depicted in a movie as a simple, helpless, and presumably sneaker-wearing old crone must not have been very appealing.

But I was relieved to see the beginning of a smile come over her face as she surveyed the secondhand, heart-shaped, picked-over gift.

"Why how nice!" she exclaimed. "Look, dear! Mr. Ward has even been good enough to open it for me."

After that encounter with Mr. Ward, we feared the worst when it came to casting the movie: something like Marjorie Main and Andy Devine as Ma and Pa Gilbreth, or, even worse, Frank Sinatra and Lana Turner as Frankie and Lillie.

As it turned out, though, Mr. Ward lost out in some sort of periodic studio upheaval, and never was connected with our movie at all. We were all very much relieved with the eventual selection of Myrna Loy and Clifton Webb. Mother met Miss Loy and liked her, and while Mr. Webb wasn't anything like Dad he was such a good actor that he brought off the part expertly. Lillie laughed out loud at the movie and, while I don't think it was exactly the way she would have staged it, she conceded when it was over that it might have been infinitely worse.

CHAPTER 20

Lifting the Calf

"I made two talks this morning," Lillie wrote me from the Philippines in 1953, where at the age of seventy-five she had undertaken a three-month teaching stint for the Institute of Public Administration there. "In the afternoon I did a taping for a broadcast that will close Girl Scout Week. Then on to the Post to have a yellow fever shot. I needed this and two for cholera. I was warned to expect a bad reaction, but I found the technique of giving the shot so excellent that it was worth experiencing.

"In the evening, I spoke at the annual meeting of Unity Church. The women all had brought chicken, rolls, and dessert. I brought the big cake I had received the day before from the Filipino Nurses Association, after carefully removing the inscription which said, 'Welcome Dr. Gilbreth.' "

Her letter the next day said, "My yellow fever shot has

given me no trouble at all. Pessimists predict a delayed reaction. Nonsense! In spite of a busy schedule, I feel too well to be bothered by such a trifle. I've just counted up my lectures and broadcasts. So far, thirty-five. We get accurate reports in the Philippine press, but they refer to me so often as the 'Adopted Mama of the Philippines' that I shudder."

She went from the Philippines to Australia on a lecture tour, and then to Formosa for a teaching job similar to that in the Philippines. Next she flew to São Paulo, Brazil, to receive a medal from the eleventh International Management Conference. Her letter of February 17, 1954, from São Paulo is typical:

"I got in early and decided to take the day off. I got a map of the city and started off . . . . Of course I got lost at every crossing, but everyone was kind, and I got pats of approval for trying.

"Then it started to pour, so I went to see some modern art. It proved to be colorful but hard to understand, though I continue to try.

"It was too wet to shop but I did get to a bookstore and buy Louis Fisher's life of Gandhi. You know me, I must have a lot of reading ahead or I starve. And I wanted to finish my studies on India before I started on Brazil."

And so it went.

When she reached her eighty-fifth birthday, we all thought it was time for her to stop her global stumping for the Gilbreth System and slow down. For one thing, she had become quite hard of hearing and always had trouble with her hearing aids. It's bad enough to travel by yourself when you're eighty-five, even if you can hear well. If you can't you're likely to get on the wrong plane or get off at the wrong airport. Once she landed at Altoona when she was trying to get to Atlanta.

She now had trouble hearing questions from the audience, after her talks. Also there had been some occasions when she hadn't been able to hear the man introducing her, and had to be nudged to get to her feet; or had started to get up before the introduction was complete, and had to be pulled down again. She even told on herself a story about how she had failed to hear a tribute paid to her by a group in Mexico City, and so had joined enthusiastically in the applause and standing ovation.

As the oldest daughter, Anne was delegated by the rest of us to try to "ground" Lillie—a job which nobody relished, but which we figured had to be done.

So when Lillie next came to visit Anne and her family in Palo Alto, California, Anne edged into the subject by saying, "Mother, did you ever consider slowing down a little and perhaps writing your memoirs?"

"Certainly I've *considered* it, dear," said Lillie, "and I may even do it one of these days. But there are so many other things I want to accomplish first."

"But you know, Mother, you are already twenty years past the usual age of retirement," Anne persisted.

"I just don't *ever* think of *that*," Lillie replied, in a tone that indicated the subject was closed.

In order to be closer to the airports, Lillie rented a small apartment in New York, although she kept her New Jersey residence, and usually went to Montclair on Sundays to go to church and have dinner with Dan or Jack and their families.

Here's where she lectured during an interval picked at random from her engagement book between June 1 and June 25, 1965, when she was eighty-seven: San Francisco, Berkeley, Carmel, Santa Cruz, and Palo Alto, all in California; Madison, Wisconsin; Feldafing am Starnberger See, Munich, and Nuremberg, Germany; Halifax, Nova Scotia; Montreal and Quebec, Canada; and Atlantic City, New Jersey. In five of these places she gave two talks, and in Munich she gave three.

And of course she still arranged her schedule so that she could combine business with family visits. She'd pop into town, distribute presents to the young fry, change her clothes, and then dash out to fulfill a speaking engagement at the Rotary Club, give a commencement address at a local college, and deliver the main talk at the annual banquet meeting of some association or other.

Some twenty-four or forty-eight hours later, she would depart, still as fresh as a daisy, flying blithely to her next overnight stop, and leaving in her wake an assortment of limply pooped descendants and their spouses.

When she visited her four unmarried sisters, who still lived together in California, they divided each day into four segments, so that they could "spell each other with Lillie."

A typical visit to Charleston, South Carolina, where I live, occurred when she was eighty-eight. She had made a couple of talks at an Air Force base in Texas the day before, and since they had a training flight going out *anyway,* she arrived here in a light bomber. There weren't any conventional stairs to get out of the thing, so the first view I had of my mother was of a pair of fairly sensible black shoes, not-too-unshapely legs, and pink to-the-knee bloomers—as she was lowered out of some sort of a hatch by two grinning officers.

Her modest enough skirt finally caught up with the rest of her. As usual she had remembered to wear something I had given her—in this case a scarf which had been a Christmas present a couple of years before. An Air Force colonel handed me the single tiny suitcase she deemed adequate, even though she planned to go directly from Charleston to Ottawa, and then San Francisco.

"She's quite a gal," he told me. "We let her take the controls part of the way. She held her real steady."

That was Lillie, all right. She didn't drive a car, but she'd try to fly a plane.

I knew all about the talk she was going to give that night at a regional banquet of the Florence Crittenton Association, because there had been some articles about it in our newspapers. But there hadn't been news stories about two other talks which, it developed, she had agreed to make. She filled me in on those as I drove to our house.

At the same time, she told me the family news. It had always been hard enough for me to keep up with which of my sisters and brothers were expecting new babies, and I found it impossible to keep up with which of the thirty grandchildren were expecting. But Lillie had it all down pat. You could put the names of all twenty great-grandchildren into a hat, pull out one of them, and she could describe the little creature right down to the last precious bicuspid.

I hope I will not be deemed deficient in filial devotion if I come right out flatly at this point and confess that I didn't like to attend my mother's speeches. I'll go even further and tell the whole embarrassing truth: I *hated* to—even more than I used to dread my father's when there was always that chance he'd do something like throw money into the audience.

Yes, given a choice between sitting in a dentist's chair or on the rostrum next to Lillie, I would have voted for the drill every time. Without Novocain, too.

It wasn't that I minded, any longer, the personal stories

she'd tell about how I thought I could save motions as a child by dodging baths. It wasn't even the fact that whoever was presiding usually felt duty-bound to ask those present if they wouldn't also like to hear a few words from "Dr. Gilbreth's son"—and they would then feel equally duty-bound to applaud me to my feet, like a *Peter Pan* audience trying to save Tinker Bell.

But what I *did* dread was the thought that Lillie wouldn't acquit herself well. Yes, she had always done a splendid job in the past. But I'd keep worrying that *this* time she'd show her age and start to ramble; that instead of sincere applause, there'd be merely polite handclapping. The very thought of it would depress me, even when I was looking forward to one of her visits.

So, for those reasons, I found excuses to skip the two daylight talks she made on that visit to Charleston. But there was no wiggling out of the Florence Crittenton talk, because three excuses would be too many.

As we drove across the Ashley River Bridge en route from my house to the Fort Sumter Hotel on Charleston's Battery where the meeting was to be held, I was frankly as nervous as a cat, and Mother seemed nervous, too.

"How did the speeches go this afternoon?" I asked her, fearing the worst.

"All right, dear, I guess," she said. "Tell me about some of the people who will be there tonight." She frowned and turned up her detested hearing aid. "Who'll introduce me?"

"A Judge Leggè will introduce you. The program director is a Mrs. Peck—her husband's a good friend of mine; he works on the newspaper, and we first met years ago when we both were reporters on the *Herald Tribune* in New York. The entertainment chairman is a Mrs. . . ."

Lifting the Calf

Lillie had closed her eyes and didn't seem to be paying the slightest attention, but I droned on anyway. It was better to talk than fidget silently.

An hour and a half later, Judge Legge had just finished introducing Lillie. Apparently the hearing aid was working, because she got up just when she was supposed to and walked to the lectern. She didn't have a manuscript or any notes. I was sitting at the head table, where I was beginning to perspire.

Lillie cleared her throat, leaned forward, and started to speak—and just at that moment the public address system started to hum.

She stepped away, and the humming stopped. Then she opened her mouth to speak again, and it started.

There was an embarrassing pause. She looked over my way in what seemed to be helpless desperation, but I didn't know how to fix it. She tried to speak again, and the humming was louder than ever.

I felt so sorry for her I wanted to get up and put an arm around her, and tell her that everything was okay, and that we'd better call it a night and go home.

But Lillie wasn't feeling sorry for herself. "You," she ordered the microphone, "hush or I'll turn you off."

The audience laughed—but it was laughing *with* her, all right.

Since the microphone wouldn't hush, Lillie *did* switch it off. And although it was her third talk of the day, you could still hear her throughout the room as she began:

"Judge Legge, I certainly appreciated that introduction. And Mrs. Peck, it's such a pleasure, in view of the long association of your husband and my son . . ." And she continued, still without a note, running down the whole list of people I had told her about, before getting into the talk it-self. I don't remember much about the content, but the *per-formance* was so remarkable that when it was over it brought down the house. Thank goodness the audience was so im-pressed that no one even thought to ask for a few anticlimactic words from Dr. Gilbreth's son.

Later, on the way back to my house, Lillie admitted she might be a little tired.

"Tired from *what?*" I needled her. "You've been sitting down almost all day long. All you've done is fly in from Texas and give three speeches."

"Do you remember what time my plane leaves tomorrow morning? Nine-something, isn't it?"

"Nine thirty-three. I'll check the airport first thing in the morning and be sure it's on time."

"You're a good boy," she nodded. "I have to be in Ottawa by three, and . . ."

"You ought to slow down," I told her firmly. "It's ridicu-lous. You ought to stay put longer. When you come to visit, you ought to stay a couple of weeks and enjoy your grand-children. You'll kill yourself."

"Didn't the talk here go all right?" she asked, and she sounded genuinely concerned. "I'd *hate* it if they just applauded me because they didn't want to hurt my feel-ings."

"Of course it went well," I reassured her. "You really had them in the aisles with that 'hush' deal, too. But why do you *do* it? Don't you think that it's time to quit and relax?"

"I suppose," she said, and for just a moment she was quite serious, "I have a 'Work, for the Night Is Coming' complex. I've felt that way ever since your father went."

"Well, that's been some forty years ago," I reminded her. It seemed strange for me to be cheering *her* up. Usually it was the other way around. "For every night that's come, there's always been a morning."

"I guess my trouble is," she admitted, patting my knee, "that I've always liked to save my time and spend my energy."

"Look, Mother," I said, "I'm not just speaking for myself. The whole family is worried about you. You're getting too old to be flying around the world by yourself and making two or three talks a day."

"And deaf as a post besides," she added for me.

"*Almost* deaf as a post," I nodded. "And you know the story about the boy who had a little bull calf, and he thought that if he lifted the calf every day, he'd finally be able to lift a full-grown bull. Well, there comes a time, dammit, when you can strain and strain, but just plain can't get the animal off the ground."

"But I lifted him again tonight, didn't I?" she asked.

"You did," I had to concede.

"And I'll lift him *tomorrow* night, too," she said.

"You probably will. And the day after tomorrow night, too. But all I'm trying to get you to realize is that you're not a spring chicken any more. Let's see, when were you born?"

She didn't answer that question, but I remembered the date, anyway. And while she tried to change the subject, I did a little mental subtraction. I'll admit it, I was amazed.

"Why, do you realize," I whinnied, "that come next May *you will be . . .*"

"Of course I realize it," she said. "And now *you* hush."

To observe Frank's one-hundredth birthday, the American Society of Mechanical Engineers and five allied organizations held a day-long Gilbreth Centennial meeting in New York December 3, 1968. Management men and old friends made speeches telling of the contributions of the Gilbreths and reminiscing about Frank's early experiments.

Lillie and all of us were there. She was frail but sharp-eyed, and could read a newspaper without glasses. She still lived alone in her New York apartment.

I sat next to her during some of the morning program. You can't whisper very well into a hearing aid—and anyway she was more interested in what was going on than in what I might have to say—so I communicated with nudges and occasional notes.

Some of Frank's original moving pictures were shown. I hadn't seen them since I was a child, and I could almost hear my Dad telling me to get going, Frank-o, and fetch your bucket of sand in case of fire.

Many of the speakers told how Gilbreth techniques still affected surgical operations, rehabilitation of the handicapped, training of the blind, library techniques, fatigue studies, and of course factory management. N. J. Ryker, the well-known space engineer, said that the principles Frank developed had been used in the design of the Apollo 8 command and service modules, which were then on the launching pad and twenty-four days later completed the historic orbit of the moon.

I nudged Lillie when he said that, and she pushed my elbow away—as if she thought it was bad manners or immodest for us to act too pleased. But then, for just a second, she looked at me, nudged me back, and smiled from ear to ear.

There was a short break before lunch, and Mother gathered her brood around her and told us she had planned for some time to retire on Dad's Centennial, and that the luncheon speech would be her last.

"I'm lifting the calf for the last time," she smiled, looking at me. She switched her gaze over to Anne. "I'm grounding myself."

An hour and a half later, she was being introduced, after a series of speakers had outlined in glowing terms her contributions to management and human relations, and her quest of Happiness Minutes and the One Best Way.

Lillie arose just a little slowly. Well, at ninety her joints had every right to be stiff. Her shoulders had rounded, but she still held her back straight. A plain hat—which would have looked just as good on backwards—helped disguise the fact that she didn't have as much hair as she used to. We all applauded her.

Her hand trembled some, as she raised it for quiet. And when the big banquet hall was finally silent, she said something in German. Then she added: "My mother used to say that. It means, 'The heart speaks loudest when the lips move not.' "

Lillie sat down. And I thought that if anyone keeps track of how many Happiness Minutes each of us tries to create in his lifetime, she must have a high score.